CONTENTS

If that's how *you* feel when you've got a Bible plonked in front of you then don't worry, **you're not alone**!

Most people don't have a *clue* where to start reading it (and that includes many **grown-ups**).

People come up come up with all sorts of weird and wonderful ways to help them pick a place to start.

For instance, there's the '**Lucky Dip**' method ...

And then there's the '**Whichever Page It Falls Open At**' method ...

Or even the '**Start At The Very Beginning And Stop At The Very End**' method ...

When it boils down to it, none of these methods is going to help you very much.

In fact, you'll probably be even *more* turned off the Bible than when you started, which is a shame, because the Bible is without a doubt the most *important* and the most *exciting* book you'll ever lay your hands on.

I reckon that what *you* need is something that's gonna help you know where's the best place to *start* so you can get the *most* out of your Bible.

HAVING TROUBLE KNOWING THE BEST PLACE TO START READING YOUR BIBLE? DON'T KNOW YOUR HEZEKIAH FROM YOUR ISAIAH? D'YOU THINK THAT MATTHEW, MARK, LUKE AND JOHN ARE ALL PART OF THE LATEST BOY BAND? IF THAT'S YOU, THEN LOOK NO FURTHER THAN THE FABULOUS NEW BORING BIBLE BOOK, 'BIBLE BUSTER'. IT'S THE ULTIMATE HANDY GUIDE TO HELP YOU GET STUCK INTO THE BIBLE WITHOUT ENDING UP A NERVOUS WRECK!

So, let's not waste any more time with the chit-chat.
On with the book!

Some Handy Hints

There's a few things you're going to need to know *before* you set about the business of *reading* the Bible.

1) Make sure you've *got* one (a Bible, that is).

The next few handy hints are going to be a little bit tricky if you *don't*.

Often as not, most homes have got one tucked away somewhere.

If you don't think you've seen one in your house *ever*, then have a go at looking for any books that look like they've never been read, or are covered in a thick layer of dust.

If you happen to stumble across a book that's not only *not* been read but is *also* is covered in a thick layer of dust, you may well have mistakenly picked up a copy of '**101 Recipes using Self-Raising Flour**'. It will be obvious to everyone's tastebuds that your mum has never bothered to open this handy book and has chosen instead to leave it lying around in the kitchen gathering cooking debris while she battles on blindly, baking your dinner by the familiar trial and error method.

OOPS! I THINK I'VE USED PLASTER MIX BY MISTAKE! OH, NEVER MIND, AT LEAST IT WILL SET FASTER!

A NOTE FROM THE PUBLISHER

The Publishers take no responsibility for the above comments and would like to take this opportunity to apologise to any mums who might have taken offence. In fact, my mum is a rather splendid cook, I'll have you know!

If you can't find anything resembling a Bible then simply ask a grown-up, point blank, if they'll *buy* you one.

They'll probably be so pleased to think you've turned over a new leaf and are already half way there to becoming a saint that they'll stump up the cash **there and then**.

Most bookshops have got some brilliant versions of the Bible designed just for kids; and, what's even *more* brilliant, they don't use words you can't understand.

VERILY, WHAT DOST THOU MEAN? I CANNOT SEE ANYTHYNGE WRONG WITH YE OLDE FASHIONED WORDES!

2) Take hold of your Bible.

We recommend using either your right hand or your left hand (or both) to perform this task. Using your feet is *not* an option (right or left – it makes no odds), particularly if you are near to a precariously perched expensive vase. This is simply *asking* for trouble, so don't even *think* about it! Similarly, taking hold of the Bible with either your mouth or your nostrils (unless you are an elephant) is *not* recommended.

Find a quiet-ish room (*without* a TV blaring out or a computer game in full swing) and make yourself comfy.

If you're gonna lie on your bed, then avoid the temptation to slip into your pyjamas and snuggle up to a hot water bottle.

You're almost *certain* to nod off – which rather defeats the object of the exercise.

I'M NOT SURE IF HE'S ABOUT TO START READING THE BOOK OF ZEPHANIAH OR IF HE'S JUST NODDED OFF!

Z-Z-Z-Z-Z-Z-Z...

4) Flick through the first few pages of your Bible until you come to the '**Contents**' page. *This* is where you it tells you where to *find* everything.

(Well when I say everything I don't mean *everything*. It won't tell you where your **Auntie** lives or for that matter the location of your **toenail collection** that mysteriously disappeared last Tuesday).

SO, THAT'S WHERE THEY WENT!

This useful bit lists *all* the books of the Bible and *where* to find them so you don't spend two weeks hunting for '**Hebrews**' in the *Old* Testament part of the Bible, only to discover that it's been hiding in the *New* Testament part all along!

You'll be using the '**Contents**' page quite a bit, so it might be worth putting a bookmark in that page when you get to it.

(Don't use your finger – we've got plenty of flicking lined up for *that* particular piece of your anatomy)

5) Now read on...

How To Use This Book

Because the Bible is packed **chocca-block** full of so much *different* stuff about all *sorts* of things we thought that it would be really handy if we broke it up into lots of *smaller* bits which each give you just a **taster** of a bit from the Bible.

That way you'll hopefully start to learn how to use the Bible, and more importantly, you'll start to get an idea what's going on. If you've got a particular liking for **blood** and **gore**...

...then you need to check out the sections on **'GRUESOME DEATHS'** or **'BLOODY BATTLES'** where you'll get potted versions of some Bible stories that feature this *sort* of thing.

If, on the other hand, you've got a rather more *sensitive* nature, then we heartily recommend making a beeline to the sections on **'Kindness'** or **'Animals'**.

(Well, *most* of the animals stories anyway - the one about sacrifices might not be *quite* so pleasant).

It's called the **'Pick a Story'** section so make sure you keep an eye out for it!

But before we get there I figure it would be a good idea to fill you in with a few essential bits of info.

First off, the Bible (if you didn't know already) is all about **God**. *He's* the one who made the universe (and everything else while he was at it).

To put it bluntly, it's *his* show!

The Bible is the book that tells us *everything* we need to know about *God*, such as...

Where he lives : Heaven.
What he's like: Powerful, Fair, Generous, Merciful.
Why he made people: So he could love us.
What he can't stand: Evil.

And heaps *more* on top of that.

The Bible's *also* the place to go if you wanna find out about the history of the world right from when things kicked off up until the end of time.

You'll be *amazed* at what you find out.

For instance, you *won't* find anything about **grunting apemen** in it *anywhere*...

And you *won't* find anything about **dinosaurs** living on earth millions of years before human beings...

Fascinating Fact:

*Did you know that the Bible mentions dinosaurs?
It doesn't actually call them that because the name wasn't
coined until the last couple of hundred years, but in the
book of Job (chapters 40 and 41) you can read about two
gi-normous and fearsome beasts that are spot-on
descriptions of dinosaur-like creatures.
Go on, check it out for yourself!*

The Bible is a right old mix of stuff with everything from **poetry**
to **prophecy** (God speaking to us through specially picked
people) and from **laws** to **letters**.

If you've read some of the *other* Boring Bible books in the series
then you'll no doubt have found out that how the Bible came
together.
(And if this *is* the first Boring Bible book you've read then
welcome on board!).

Put simply, God inspired (gave the ideas to) a whole *variety* of people from **different places** and over a **long period of time** with precisely what *he* wanted to go into the Bible.
Nothing more, nothing less! Amazingly, when it was all put together, everything fitted *perfectly*..

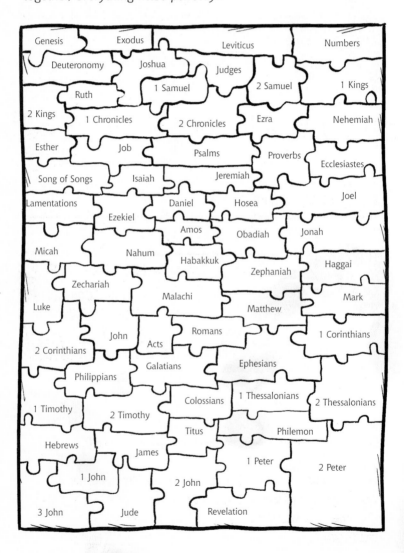

Alive and Kicking!

Did you know that the Bible is **alive**?

Well it is, which means that whenever you read it *something* extraordinary could happen.

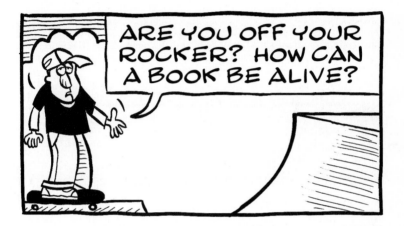

Let me explain...

The Bible is sometimes called '**God's Word**'.

The reason for this is quite simple.

It's because they're the *words* that *God* wants to say to us.

(That wasn't too complicated was it?)

So, whenever we get stuck into reading the Bible we should expect God to actually speak to us through what we're reading.

How does *that* happen?

Here's how...

Here's how number one: The person who gave the writers of the Bible their brilliant ideas was none other than the **Holy Spirit** himself.

If you're not sure who *he* is, then get yourself a copy of Boring Bible book *Hyper Holy Happenings* and all will be revealed!

In a word, the Holy Spirit is **God**.

Here's how number two: When you become a Christian you get the Holy Spirit to come and live *inside* of you (check out Boring Bible book *Crazy Christians* - sorry about all the ads).

Here's how number three: Because the Holy Spirit is the *author* of the Bible (it was his idea, after all) then when you read it (and you've got the Holy Spirit living inside of you) then *he* can bring it to life as you read it and show you what it means and how it can affect your life.

Is that good or is that **good**?!

One *last* thing (before we dive head first into all the Bible bits)
is **how** to track things down in the Bible once you've found a bit
that takes your fancy.

Okay! You'll need to get your imaginations fired up for this one.
I want you to imagine that the Bible is like a bookshelf and on
that bookshelf are **66** books.

Oh, go on then. Have a pretty little picture if it'll help you ...

... and *each* of these books is *one* of the books that make up the
Bible like **Genesis** or **Revelation**.

(For your information, they're the first and last books.)

If I told you to look up **Genesis chapter 7** then, just like you
would with an ordinary book, you'd go to **Genesis** and flick
through until you've found **chapter 7**.

(Take a look for yourself and find which famous sailor is
featured in *this* bit of the Bible).

To make life easy for you, each chapter is divided up into verses.

(They don't rhyme, but don't let *that* put you off.)

If I tell you to find **Genesis chapter 7 verse 6** then all *you've*
gotta do is run your finger down the page until you get to a
little number **6**.

(**Be warned!** You'll need your
swimming gear when you
get to it).

And that's all there is to it.

Easy peasy!

I'M READY?

So that's about all you need to know to get started.

What's coming up *next* is the '**Pick a Story**' page (or should I say *pages* – there's so much stuff there's no way that we can cram it *all* onto just *one* page).

Cast your eye over them and you'll see all the *different* sorts of Bible bits we've picked out for you.

(Aren't we considerate?)

To be honest, it was really hard choosing *which* bits to put in. but hopefully there's a nice little selection to please *everyone* ...

Well – almost *everyone*!

Once you've found a section that takes your fancy, look it up, check out the lowdown on what's it's all about, and then have a go at finding the bit in a *real* Bible so you can see if we've told you the *whole* story or if we've missed something out.

Okay, **get to it**!

Pick a Story Page(s)

BAD MOVES

King David was the main man in Israel and for *once* he decided to take a break from leading the **Israelite army** to war. (Did he just fancy a year off? Well, that's *anyone's* guess). While his troops were busily slaughtering their enemies (the **Ammonites** on this *particular* occasion) David was lounging around his rather nice palace. *That's* where the trouble started. After catching forty winks he went up onto the **roof** to get a **bird's eye view** of the city (**Jerusalem**). But he got a lot *more* than he bargained for! He clapped eyes on a lady called **Bathsheba** taking a bath (you'll have to work *that* one out for yourself) and wasted no time in having her brought to the palace so he could make love to her. What was *worse* was that Bathsheba's hubbie, **Uriah the Hittite**, was one of King David's *own* soldiers and was busily killing Israel's enemies while all *this* was going on.

The long and the short of it was that King David did his darnedest to cover his tracks, but the *more* he tried the *worse* he made things.

God was having *none* of it and David got his come-uppance. To find out *what* that was and to see what happened to poor old cheated-upon Uriah, you're gonna have to go to **2 Samuel** and read all of **chapter 11**. (Don't worry, it's not *that* long!).

OH, DEAR! I HOPE URIAH THE HITTITE DOESN'T TAKE AFTER HIS NAME!

BAD MOVES

Ananias and Sapphira went to the same church as Jesus's best mate, Peter, (you know, the guy who had a go at walking on the water but sank) which meant that they were right where it was happening as far as miracles, healings and all *that* sort of stuff was concerned. God was doing so *many* brilliant things that nobody gave a *second thought* for themselves. They were more concerned with seeing more and more people becoming Christians (which they did in their *thousands*!). Everyone shared *everything* they owned so that *no-one* went without a thing. *That's* where Ananias and his wife came in. They decided to **sell some property** so that the money could be given to the less well off people in the church.

All okay *so* far.

What they *didn't* tell anybody was that they had planned to keep *some* of the proceeds from the sale for *themselves*.

Not *quite* so okay!

What they *hadn't* banked on was God **blowing the whistle** on their **evil scheming**.

Their fate can be discovered in **Acts chapter 5** and from **verses 1 through to 11**.

GOOD MOVES

Do you wanna be **rich and famous** while you're still young? Then it might be worth taking a leaf out of **King Solomon's** book (not literally of course – we don't want to appear to be encouraging vandalism now, do we?). Solomon's dad had been King David but now it was *Solomon's* turn to rule **Israel**. The *good news* was that he made no bones about his love for God (*just* like his dad). As far as *Solomon* was concerned **God came first** and *that* was the end of it. But being king was a whopping great responsiblity for a young man and Solomon knew it.

One night, while Solomon was asleep, he had a dream (which I suppose is the best time to have one).

In the dream God appeared to him and asked him the following question ...

There's a question and a half.

What do you think *your* answer would be?

Read **1 Kings chapter 3 verses 1 to 15** and you'll see *what* Solomon asked God for.

DINOSAURS

Most of us know a thing or two about **dinosaurs** don't we? There's been enough films and TV programmes about them to keep a dinosaur fan happy for the rest of their life. But how do we *know* what dinosaurs looked like? Well, that's easy. Using their fossilised bones as a starting point, scientists can recreate these huge creatures with a great deal of accuracy. Which is *why* we know that some of the land-based dinosaurs had *gi-normous* tails, legs like *tree trunks* and *amazing strength*.

And dinosaurs didn't just limit themselves to dry ground.
The **seas** were home to many large dinosaur-like creatures as well.

With their huge bodies they powered their way through the waters as **kings of the oceans**.

But what you most probably *didn't* know was that the Bible describes **two very big beasts** which sound *exactly* like the sort of dinosaurs we've just been describing.

Don't believe me?
Check out **Job chapters 40 verses 15 to 24** and **Job chapter 41** all the way through to the end.

And while you're at it, why not have a go at drawing a *picture* of what the Bible describes and then compare it with some of the pictures in your dinosaur books.

KINGS

If you've read Boring Bible book *Catastrophic Kings* then you'll be well aware what a hit and miss affair the **kings of Israel** and **Judah** were. The guy in the story I'm about to tell you about fell fair and square into the '**miss**' category. He went by the name of **Zimri** so he was probably *already* well cheesed-off by always being last every time in the school register. Whether that excuses his actions is another matter! Zimri had done pretty well for himself and was in charge of *half* of king Elah's chariots...

BETWEEN YOU AND ME, I WOULDN'T MIND BEING IN CHARGE OF THE OCCASIONAL WHOLE CHARIOT!

...but that just wasn't *enough* for the **ambitious Zimri**. While the king was busily getting himself drunk, Zimri seized his chance and **assassinated Elah**. Not content with his bloody deed, Zimri *then* went and bumped off *every* male member of Elah's family (including Elah's best mates!).

Seeing that there was now a **vacancy** for **king of Israel**, Zimri made quick work of filling the position *himself*.

Unfortunately, not *everyone* was quite so chuffed with Zimri's speedy social climbing.

To find out who *didn't* like what he'd done and how *long* he ruled Israel, go and look up the story in **1 Kings chapter 16** and from **verse 8** right through to **verse 20**.

Here's a clue: Zimri's claim to fame was that he was Israel's **shortest** ruler (and I don't mean a 2-inch one!).

KINGS

If you've ever read the story of David and Goliath then here's some *more* of the same. **King Hezekiah** is our main man but as we join him he's got his back against the wall (not literally, of course!). The **Assyrian army** are all set to attack the city of **Jerusalem** and things aren't looking good for its quivering inhabitants.

The powerful Assyrian army have been undefeated all season and Jerusalem is *next* on their hit list.

Hezekiah is right in the thick of it and he's getting *desperate*. The Assyrians are giving him a hard time and taunting him something rotten. Being a good (and sensible) king he cried out to **God** for help.

And here are the highlights of the message God gave Hezekiah to give to the Assyrians (and their emperor, Sennacherib) ...

THE CITY OF JERUSALEM LAUGHS AT YOU SENNACHERIB...YOU HAVE BEEN DISRESPECTFUL TO ME, THE HOLY GOD OF ISRAEL...I KNOW EVERYTHING ABOUT YOU...I KNOW HOW YOU RAGE AGAINST ME...I WILL PUT A HOOK THROUGH YOUR NOSE AND TAKE YOU BACK BY THE SAME ROAD YOU CAME.

That very night, without Hezekiah's army lifting a finger, God **wiped out** the best part of the Assyrian army. Read **2 Kings chapters 18** and **19** for the *whole* exciting story of how trusting God **100%** can make you a winner *every* time but how trying to *take on* God is one **big, big mistake**. It might be a couple of chapters but it's a brilliant story, and you'll also find out *exactly* how many Assyrian soldiers were killed by God in **one fell swoop**.

QUEENS

Do you want to get a whole **book** of the Bible named after you? Well you've gotta do something pretty special, that's all I can say. Esther, or **Queen Esther** as she eventually became, was quite a lady! Her people (the **Jews**) had been conquered and carted off to Persia (because they'd turned their backs on God). She was an orphan so her good old uncle **Mordecai** brought her up instead. **King Xerxes**, who ruled the land, was on the hunt for a *new* queen after Queen Vashti had turned stroppy on him. After a nationwide search, Esther got the job.

Every good story has to have a **baddie** and *this* one is no exception. Our baddie was none other than **Haman**, the **Prime Minister**.

Haman was an arrogant so-and-so and when Mordecai refused to bow down to him (he reserved *that* sort of thing for God) Haman was *well miffed*. From that moment on Haman had it in for Mordecai

I'M NOT ALL BAD I'LL HAVE YOU KNOW – I ALWAYS TRY TO AVOID STEPPING ON INSECTS!

and, for that matter, for **every single Jew in Persia**.

He was so **mad** that he persuaded King Xerxes to **kill them all**. Well, the long and the short of it is that Queen Esther put her neck on the line and stood up for her fellow Jews (hooray!). From there on in, Haman's dastardly plans **backfired** on him big time. Not only *didn't* the Jewish people get destroyed, but Mordecai *didn't* end up getting hanged on Haman's specially built gallows either.

Who got the chance to test the gallows out instead? Check out the book of **Esther chapter 7** to find out.

QUEENS

Where do you go to in the Bible if you want to find out about a famous queen? Yep, the book of **Kings**!!!! (Nice one!). The lady in question isn't really the star of the show but it's queens you want so it's queens we shall give you.

The **Queen of Sheba** trekked all the way from Arabia (1,200-ish miles) to call on King Solomon, who was getting a bit of a name for himself for his **wisdom** and his **wealth** (not forgetting his **wives** – but that's *another* story!).

She turned up with **armfuls of prezzies** for Solomon (spices, jewels, gold) so it's a good job she didn't catch a plane (if they'd been invented) or she'd have been well over the limit on her hand luggage allowance.

A PLANE'S NOT SUCH A BAD IDEA!

The **Queen of Sheba** wasn't the least bit jealous of Solomon; in fact, she went as far as to give **all the credit to God** for the way he'd doled out so much good stuff to Israel's King.

The way the *Bible* tells it, you can see that the Queen was completely bowled over by what she heard and saw.

If you look up **1 Kings chapter 10** (the first **13 verses**) then you can read the *whole* story.

Run your finger down to **verse 13** and you'll discover whether the camels had an easier time of it on the *return* journey.

RESCUES

Before you get stuck into *this* story, be warned: this is not the *normal* way to get out of jail. What am I talking about? Well, *this* rescue features not only a well-known disciple of Jesus (**Peter**) but also a **prison**. That's where Peter ended up courtesy of **King Herod** who wasn't *too* partial to the likes of Peter forever going on about **Jesus** in public places. Things weren't looking good for Peter. One of the other disciples, **James**, had already been **executed** for the *same* 'crime' so it looked like Peter's days were numbered.

The night before his trial Peter was fast asleep when he had an unexpected visitor ...

MUM, GREAT TO SEE YOU!

Er. not quite!

More like an **angel from God**.

Once Peter had come to, the angel ordered Peter to get dressed and then follow him. The Bible actually says that Peter wasn't sure whether this was for real or if it was some kind of **vision** he was having. I mean, the guards didn't even **bat an eyelid**!

It was nothing short of a **miracle**.

When Peter turned up at the house of his friends who were praying for his rescue do you think *they* believed what had happened?

Well, read **Acts chapter 12** right through to **verse 19** to see what *their* reaction was.

DREAMS

Just about *everyone* has dreams but the dream **Nebuchadnezzar**, the king of **Babylon** had was one you'd be *quite* happy to forget. He was *so* frightened by his dream that he summoned all his magicians and the like and demanded that they tell him its **meaning**. Unfortunately, they were next to useless. The dream, which featured **a tall tree being cut down**, had them well and truly *stumped* (no joke intended!). There was nothing for it but to call for good old **Daniel** (famous for his overnight stay in a den of lions). Daniel had relocated to Babylon (from Israel) some time back (mainly due to the small matter of the Babylonians attacking Israel and taking loads of them back as slaves). Daniel was a man who relied on **God**, so God had given him the ability to understand dreams, which included the rather disturbing dream that was troubling bad King Nebuchadnezzar. In short, the dream was a message from God to let the proud and arrogant king know that *he* wasn't the boss – *God* was. And until the king got round to acknowledging that useful bit of info he was going to be **cut down to size** (like the tree). What Daniel said, happened. The king went **loopy**, left the palace and went to live outside like an animal ...

Daniel chapter 4 from **verse 34 to 37** will reveal whether Nebuchadnezzar learned his lesson from the dream.

DREAMS

I'll bet you've heard about the famous dreamer in *this* Bible bit. Yep, it's none other than **Joseph** (but without his coloured coat – that's long gone). Our hero has got himself in a bit of a pickle (through no fault of his own) and ended up in an **Egyptian prison**. Not to worry, he's got the king of Egypt's wine steward and his baker to keep him company...

Luckily for Joseph they *also* enjoyed sleeping.
One night (so the Bible tells us) they *both* had a **dream**.
Nothing unusual about *that*, you're probably thinking, and you'd be right. Fortunately, or unfortunately (depending on which of the two we're talking about) their dreams predicted what was going to *happen* to them.
The wine steward had a dream about **grapes** (what a surprise!) and the baker had a dream about **bread** (even *less* of a surprise!).
Track down **Genesis chapter 40** for the *complete* story, but if you just want to find out who had the happy ending (and who *didn't*) then skip to **verses 20** through to **23**.

ANIMALS

If you're either **squeamish** or if you're an **animal** (or if you're *both*) then this page is definitely *not* recommended reading! What we're looking at here is stuff from the Bible book **Leviticus** and it's all to do with **sacrifices**. *Animal* sacrifices to be precise. If you've read any of the *other* Boring Bible books you might well have come across the word '**sin**'. Okay, so it's an itty bitty word but the Bible says it's a **big thing** with God. Why? Because sin means doing things God says you *shouldn't* do. The **Israelites** (as featured in Leviticus) kept messing up (sinning) for which the punishment should have been **death**! But 'cos God's kind he gave them a way out. He told them that if they killed an animal *instead* then that would do the trick. A life for a life was how God saw it. But you couldn't just go killing animals **willy nilly**...

There was a *proper* way to do it (as set out by God) and even *then* it was a job only the specially picked **priests** could do. Check out **Leviticus chapter 4 verses 3** to **12** and see if *you'd* have had the stomach to be a priest.
(I'll warn you now – it's **bloodthirsty** stuff!)

ANIMALS

Here's a question for you. **Can animals talk?** I don't mean the sort of mimicking that *parrots* do. I mean the sort of talking where the animal has some sort of an idea *what* it's saying. Well, unless it was in **Shrek** or something like *that* (and this *isn't* a book about films so you can forget that train of thought) you'd probably say **no**. But what we've got here, in *this* bit from the Bible is a **real live** talking donkey. Nope, I'm not kidding! The *whole* story is a bit of a whopper so you're just gonna get the edited highlights. To cut a very long story short, there's this prophet called **Balaam** who's been summoned by **King Balak** (a king of Moab) to rain down curses on the approaching Israelites (who they were scared stiff of). Balaam

didn't particularly want the job because he knew that God was on the *Israelites'* side and opposing God was not the *best* of ideas.

King Balak sent his top brass to fetch Balaam to fulfill his task but on the way something **strange** happened.

Balaam was riding on his

I'VE SUDDENLY GONE OFF THE IDEA OF BEING A PROPHET!

donkey when **three times** an angel from God blocked the road. Unfortunately, only the terrified *donkey* could see him. Balaam beat the donkey with his stick to get it to keep moving but **nothing doing** – the donkey dug its heels in and wasn't going *anywhere*. That made Balaam even *madder*.

And then, as I hinted earlier, something rather unusual happened which you can look up in **Numbers chapter 22** and from **verse 28** to **35**.

If you've got a brother than *this* is the story for you!

We're heading right back to the **beginning of time** to check out the lowdown on the world's *first ever* brothers – **Cain** and **Abel**. Let's be honest, things were pretty cool for these boys, after all their mum and dad were none other than **Adam** and **Eve**, the world's **first two people**. So, what we've got *here* is one top **celebrity household** ...

THEY MIGHT BE FAMOUS BUT I DON'T THINK MUCH OF THEIR DRESS SENSE!

But Cain and Abel weren't a couple of spoilt rich kids. No way! These boys *worked* for a living.

Cain was a **farmer** and his little bruvver, Abel, was a **shepherd**. One day, Abel did something you'll read a lot about in the Boring Bible books – he made a **sacrifice** to God by killing the first lamb to be born and giving the **best** parts to God.

Cain *also* brought an offering to God but *he* decided just to settle for some of the stuff he'd grown in the field.

The Bible says that God *accepted* Abel's gift because it was given in faith but *rejected* Cain's because it was given with the **wrong heart** which made big bruvver **very mad indeed**.

Want to find out how *not* to settle scores with your brother? Read **Genesis chapter 4** and **verse 8**.

GUYS

Let me introduce you to **Peter**. This guy *really* made the big time. One day he was nothing more than a **simple fisherman**, trawling the shores of Galilee in Israel ...

LESS OF THE SIMPLE, IF YOU PLEASE!

and the *next* he was one of **Jesus's** disciples. Peter stuck with Jesus through thick and thin but when Jesus *finally* got arrested for upsetting the religious leaders in Israel, Peter did what every loyal friend would do ... **he played dumb**.

While Jesus was being cross-examined Peter was hanging around in the shadows trying to figure out what to do.

"This man was with Jesus!" "You are one of them too!"

"There isn't any doubt that this man was with Jesus!"

Peter was cornered (and scared) and he blurted out that he wasn't *anything* to do with Jesus – in fact, just like Jesus had said he would.

Peter was torn apart by **guilt** at denying Jesus; but have a look in **John chapter 21 verse 15** through to **verse 17**.

It's after Jesus has been executed and then raised to life again by God. Jesus turns up (amazingly) and makes a **barbecue** for the disciples (*including* Peter). But even *more* amazingly, he gives Peter a **second chance**. Peter had said **three times** that he didn't know Jesus, so how many times does Jesus ask Peter if he loves him? Go on, read it and see how fantastic Jesus is at forgiving us.

GUYS

Would you give away *everything* you had for a hot meal (even a quadruple chicken, cheese and ketchup burger)? Nope, me neither. Which is why the two fellas under the Boring Bible spotlight are of interest to us. Meet **Esau** and **Jacob**. Their *grandad* was **Abraham** (founder of Israel) and their dad was **Isaac** (who for your info was 60 – yes **60**! – when they were born).

Esau and Jacob were **twins** and even *before* they'd popped out of their mum (Rebecca's) tum they were at each other's throats or rather *heels*. Red, hairy Esau (no I'm not being personal – that's what the Bible says) came out *first* followed by Jacob, who was gripping Esau's **heel**.

You're gonna have to read up a lot more than this *one* story to discover what a running battle this pair had all through their lives, but the '**stew story**' will give you a good idea that all was *not* sweetness and light!

Esau had been out hunting and had worked up a good appetite, so it was a stroke of luck that Jacob had just cooked lunch as he charged in.

Jacob was cooking everybody's favourite food...'**red stuff**'. Well, at least that's what *Esau* called it...

What's the **price** for a bowl of '**red stuff**'?
Genesis chapter 25 verses 27 to **34** will reveal all.
(Service charge *not* included)

GALS

Calling all twelve year old girls! This page is dedicated to to *you*. (Aren't we kind?). Why? 'Cos, surprise, surprise, it's all about a **twelve year old girl**. If you know anything at all about **Jesus** you'll know that he was *big* on **miracles**. And *this* Bible bit is no exception. We join Jesus just as he's just returned from a boat trip and boy! is there *some* welcoming committee. The crowds had turned out in force to see what he'd do next. But there was one man in the crowd who definitely *wasn't* there to watch. His name was **Jairus**, and his daughter was on her **death bed**. He begged Jesus to come and heal her. Jesus saw that Jairus **believed** he could do it, so he headed out to his house.
Too late!
The girl was **dead** and the house was filled with weeping and wailing mourners.
That didn't stop Jesus.
He cleared the place of *everyone* but the mum and dad and three of his disciples ...

SPOILSPORTS! I WAS JUST GETTING INTO MY WAILING!

Jesus simply told the little girl to "get up" and guess what ... she *did*!
Jesus had one *last* command to give and you can find it at the very end of the story, which is in **Mark chapter 5** from **verse 21** to **43**.

GALS

You want to hear about a **gutsy** lady? Then let me intoduce you to **Deborah**. Just to set the scene, we're in Israel but things aren't looking too good for the Israelites (God's special people). They'd been conquered by the **Canaanites** who were cruel and violent. If you've read Boring Bible book *Catastrophic Kings* then you'll know all about how, whenever the Israelites (at this point in their history) turned back to God, he gave them a new leader (called a '**judge**'). *That's* what Deborah was. So the Bible tells us, she used to sit under a palm tree and make **wise** decisions. She was also a **prophet**, which meant she listened to God and told the people what God was saying.

On this *particular* occasion God was saying that he'd heard their cries for help and was going to give them **victory** over the Canaanites.

Not *everyone* in Israel was made of the same stuff as Deborah. **Barak**, who was in charge of the attack, wouldn't go unless Deborah went with him ...

As it happened, it was a resounding success but *Deborah* got all the credit (quite right too!). Have a look at **Judges chapter 4** from **verse 17** to the end of the chapter to see a very **gory** ending to this Bible bit. (**If you dare!**).

GALS

When it comes to the fame game, **Ruth** really comes out tops. Not *only* does she get a **whole book** of the Bible named after her (not a bad feat when there's only **66** up for grabs) but she *also* gets to be in **Jesus's family tree** (check out **Matthew chapter 1 verse 5**). So, who *was* this amazing gal?

Well, she starts out as a bit of a *nobody* (which means there's hope for the *rest* of us) from the land of **Moab**. Her fortunes change when she gets married to one of **Naomi's** boys (they're Israelites but living in Moab – don't ask me why, there's not enough time). Naomi's hubbie *and* her boys eventually die (sob!), so she decides it's time to go back to Israel. Guess who decides to stick with her mother-in-law? Yep, loyal **Ruthie**. Not only does she go *with* Naomi but she *worships* **Israel's God** (wise decision).

Everyone's pleased to see Naomi back and none more so than her rich relative, **Boaz**.

Ruth's loyalty and faithfulness was well rewarded when Boaz offered to make Ruth his wife – which she became.

There's only four chapters to Ruth so you could whiz through the story in no time, but for now, look up **Ruth chapter 4, verse 17** and you can see *which* famous king of Israel Ruth was the **great grandma** of. Here's a clue ...

TOILETS

I'll bet you're thinking that this is a bit of a wind-up. aren't you? **Toilets** in the Bible? Whatever *next*? Well you'd be *wrong*, 'cos the brill thing about the Bible is that it *always* tells it like it is, as you will *soon* discover.

A quick bit of background. We're in **Israel** and a guy called **Saul** is king; the *bad* news is that he's making a bit of a hash of it.

Not to worry, God's got a replacement waiting in the wings by the name of **David**.

God *likes* David. The people of Israel *like* David.

But Saul **hates** him!

In fact he hated him *so much* that he wanted him **dead.**

With the help of **three thousand** of his best fighting men Saul set off in hot pursuit.

David and his band of men were holed up in a cave when they had an unexpected visitor ... **King Saul**.

Saul was unaware that he had an audience, which is just as well because the Bible says he went in there to **relieve** himself (very politely put).

David and his men *could* have seized their chance and killed Saul there and then, but a quick scan down **1 Samuel chapter 24 verses 4** through to **7** will tell you what *really* happened.

SOMETHING FISHY!

If you like *short* Bible bits then have we got a short one for you? How does **four verses** sound? Hmm, perhaps a bit on the lazy side, eh? Never mind, what you *lose* on size you *gain* in quality. You not only get a nice big **shot** of teaching but you also get a **miracle** thrown in for good measure. Good or what?!

What we've got is **Jesus** being quizzed by some **religious bigwigs** in charge of collecting **taxes** for Israel's temple.

As usual they were trying to trick Jesus into saying something *against* their religion. They *should* have known better – they *always* seemed to end up with **egg on their faces** when they went down this road...

Jesus knew their game and, rather than appear to be flouting their petty traditions, he played ball and paid up his temple tax, just as they asked.

What they *weren't* expecting was his **method of payment**.

Jesus sent Peter (a disciple) off with a rod and line to do a spot of **fishing**.

I'm sure you can summon up the energy to read the four easy peasy verses in **Matthew chapter 17 verses 24** to **27** to see what exactly it was that Peter **hooked**.

SOMETHING FISHY!

I'll bet most of you don't mind munching your way through some fish every now and then. What's *not* so tasty is a having a fish munching its way through *you*. That's sort of what happened to the star of this **fishy tale**. **Jonah** is his name and he was a **prophet**, which meant that God had a message he wanted Jonah to deliver. This wasn't a singing telegram sort of message. *Nothing* so pleasant. God wanted Jonah to tell the people of **Nineveh** that he was calling time on their **wicked ways**. If they didn't change, then it was goodbye Nineveh.

Jonah figured that his message would be *ignored* and that God *wouldn't* carry out his threat of **destruction**, so he decided to do a runner.

Big mistake!

He caught a **ship to Spain** but God brought about such a terrible storm that there was nothing for it but to chuck Jonah (who the sailors thought was the cause of the storm) overboard. Guess what? The storm stopped. Did Jonah drown? Nope! A huge **fish** gulped him down and gave him a roof over his head for **three days**.

And then, to add insult to injury, the fish *spat* Jonah ashore in none other than ... (yep, you guessed it) ... **Nineveh**.

Jonah *reluctantly* did the job God had assigned him and *amazingly* the people of Nineveh turned away from their wickedness.

How long did God give the people of Nineveh to repent?

Jonah chapter 3 verse 4 has your answer.

SOMETHING FISHY!

If you know *anything* about Jesus then you're sure to know that *some* of his disciples were **fishermen**. After Jesus's resurrection (when he came back to life) he appeared to lots of different people. *One* of those times was when Peter and some of the other disciples were out on a **fishing trip**. They'd probably not been fishing for *ages*. Following Jesus around had taken up *all* their time. Now, with time on their hands, while they waited to know what to do *next*, they pushed their boat out to sea and lowered their nets. They were out **all night** but caught absolutely **zilch**!

With the sun coming up, they caught sight of somebody on the shore and he was calling out instructions to them.

It was **Jesus** and when they cast their nets on the other side of the boat (as he was telling them) they pulled in a **whopper of a haul**.

Jesus already had a **barbecue** going so they had a great breakfast. I wonder if they'd remembered that Jesus had once told them that they would be **fishers of men**, and that *this* miracle was to encourage them to see that working with Jesus they could expect a **big catch**?

Have a **trawl** through the story in **John chapter 21 verses 1** through to **14** and see if you can find out how *many* fish they actually caught.

JEALOUSY

How do you feel if someone at school does really well at something and they are everyone's *favourite* person? You're **pleased** for them, aren't you? You're not? You're not just the teensiest bit *jealous* are you? Well if you *are*, then you'd be in jolly good company.

King Saul has had it up to *here* (forehead height) with **David**. Everything is David *this* and David *that*.

He's *well* cheesed-off and *now* he's put the cherry on the cake by **killing Goliath** the Philistine giant.

King Saul had ventured out to join the crowds welcoming David and the Israelite army back. I'll bet he wish he *hadn't*.

The place was *swarming* with joyful crowds singing and dancing. And here's what the women were singing ...

Saul was so **seethingly jealous** that the very next day he went **berserk**.

While David attempted to sooth his king with a bit of his famous **harp playing** (was there *no* end to his talents?) Saul was reaching for his **spear** which he hurled at David.

Did David end up skewered by Saul's spear or did he live to pluck another day?

1 Samuel chapter 18 verses **10** and **11** will tell.

STRANGE BUT TRUE!

You've probably heard of **Joshua** before, haven't you? He's the one who led the **Israelites** to walk round the city of **Jericho** before its walls came tumbling down. *This* Bible bit has got *another* fantastic **show-stopping** miracle to amaze you. Joshua and the Israelites are working their way through **Canaan** (the land God had given them to live in) clearing out its wicked inhabitants. Along the way they'd made peace with the **Gibeonites** and all was going well. The *other* people living into the land were a bit miffed with the Gibeonites for giving in so easily so they decided to attack them (and why not?)

With Gibeon encircled by invading armies they sent word to Joshua to come and rescue them – which he did.

Joshua and his army mounted a surprise night attack which scared the invaders silly. To make things *worse*, God sent down the world's **biggest hailstones** to stop them running off (killing more than the Israelite army).

I THINK I'M GONNA ASK FOR A REFUND!

And just so they could finish the job off *properly*, Joshua commanded the **sun** and the **moon** to stay still until the enemy had all been completely destroyed (giving them extra daylight). So, for how *long* did the sun stand still?

Check it out in **Joshua chapter 10 verse 13**.

STRANGE BUT TRUE!

The Bible is **chocca-block** *full* of some amazing miracles but the one we're about to look at **knocks spots** off the *lot* of them. Here's what's been occurring. **Jesus** (God's Son) has just been executed (on the Friday) and it's now Sunday. Jesus' burial had been a bit of a **rush job** to get it done before the Jewish Sabbath (rest day) started and there hadn't been time to cover the body with perfumes and spices as was the tradition. When a group of ladies turned up at the tomb to prepare Jesus's body they had a bit of a surprise. (Understatement of the year!). They were greeted by a couple of **shining angels** and more strangely ... **an empty tomb**.

How did they *know* it was empty? Easy. The tomb stone had been conveniently rolled back to reveal *all* ...

WHY ARE YOU LOOKING AMONG THE DEAD FOR ONE WHO IS ALIVE? HE IS NOT HERE, HE HAS BEEN RAISED.

Jesus had always said that his death wouldn't be the end and he'd been right.

So *where* was Jesus? Had he gone straight back to heaven where he'd come from? **Luke chapter 24** will solve the mystery.

STRANGE BUT TRUE!

One thing you'll learn as you get stuck into the Bible is that God isn't only interested in doing spectacularly **big** miracles like parting the Red Sea so that the Israelites could pass through. He's *also* on call to do 'mini' miracles (if you know what I mean). Which leads me nicely in to a *mini* story from the Bible featuring a prophet called **Elisha** (not to be confused with *Elijah*, who was his boss). Elisha headed up a whole *team* of prophets but they had a bit of an **accommodation crisis** – the place they lived in was too cramped. Nothing for it but to build something **bigger**. Elisha gave them the go-ahead to chop down some of the trees by the river Jordan.

HEY! NOW WE'VE GOT AN ACCOMMODATION CRISIS!

All was going well until ... **PLOP!**
Oops! One of the **axe-heads** had fallen into the water and the prophet using it only had it on **loan**. What was he to *do*?
Elisha to the rescue!
Our prophet hero found out where it had fallen and then did the most *unusual* thing, but rather than spoil it for you I'm going make you do a bit of investigating in **2 Kings chapter 6** and from **verse 1** through to **verse 7**. Happy investigating!

STRANGE BUT TRUE!

Did you know that there's **graffiti** in the Bible? Well let's head back to ancient **Babylon** where **Belshazzar** is king. His dad, **Nebuchadnezzar**, had made the *big* mistake of getting too big for his boots and even thinking he was *bigger* than **God**! Nebuchadnezzar had wised up and humbled himself before God but *not so* his **proud** son. Belshazzar was about to get his come-uppance and it happened right in then middle of a **mega banquet** he'd thrown for a **thousand noblemen**. Belshazzar decided to impress his guests by bringing out all the gold and silver cups and bowls his dad had captured from God's Temple in Israel. **Bad move!** As the wicked king started to praise the *made-up* gods of gold, silver, bronze, iron, wood and stone, a **human hand** appeared and began **writing** on the plaster wall of the palace.

Here's what the hand wrote ...

Unfortunately, nobody had the *foggiest* idea what **Mene, Mene, Tekel, Parsin** actually *meant*.

Not the **magicians**, not the **wizards**, not the **astrologers**. Fortunately, Belshazzar's mum suddenly remembered about Daniel who could interpret things. **Daniel chapter 5, verses 25 to 28** will tell you what it meant and **verse 29 to 31** will reveal the *fate* of the proud king.

STRANGE BUT TRUE!

Ever wished you could skip swimming lessons and just **walk on water** instead? Well just put *that* thought to the back of your mind. To do something like *that* you've gotta have **bigtime faith** (and preferably be the **Son of God)** which rules out everybody *except* **Jesus**. Which is a bit of a coincidence 'cos that's who *this* Bible bit is all about.

Jesus had had a hectic day **teaching** and **doing miracles**. What he needed *most* was some time out with his **Father** in heaven. First off he dispatched his disciples to sail across the lake ready for the next day's work and then he settled down to **pray**.

That night a storm blew up on the lake and the boat was tossed left, right and centre.

Some time between three and six in the morning *Jesus* turned up – **just like that!** He'd walked across the stormy sea and was now *level* with the boat. Were the disciples pleased to see him? No, they were **terrified**! They thought Jesus was a **ghost**. It was only when Jesus *spoke* that they realised *who* he was.

As soon as Jesus got into the boat the wind died down.

Oh yes. I've missed a bit out. Jesus wasn't the *only* one who walked on water that night. I wonder who *else* had a go, and for that matter *how* he got on? The story's in **Matthew chapter 14** and covers verses **22** to **33**.

STRANGE BUT TRUE!

One thing you'll hopefully realise as you check out the Bible is that because God is God of the whole *universe* then if you're on speaking terms with him there's absolutely *nothing* whatsoever he can't do for you. And **Hezekiah** is a king who's about to prove it. He was one of Israel's *good* kings but he was a bit poorly ...

POORLY? I'M ABOUT TO DIE!

Okay, he was very, *very*, poorly. Will *that* do? Good!
Hezekiah wept before God and **pleaded** to be **healed**.
Isaiah the prophet was acting as a sort of go-between for Hezekiah and God and came back with the good news that God had granted him another **fifteen years** of life.
Just to make *certain* in his own mind that he didn't need to get his house in order *quite* yet the king asked God for some sort of **sign**.
The sign God gave was that the **shadow** of the sun would go **back** up the stairway **ten steps**. Imagine God making the sun move *back* in space for **one man**! Amazing!
If you're nosey enough to want to know what embarrassing ailment was afflicting Hezekiah, then flick to **2 Kings chapter 20** and **verse 7**. Sounds **painful**!

ANGELS

Have you ever wondered *how* God manages to answer so *many* prayers all in one go? Well *one* reason is that he's **God** which means he's capable of doing *huge* amounts of stuff without *any* effort. But God's *also* got a massive **workforce** who he sends to earth to do what he tells them. These *particular* messengers are called **angels** and they're *everywhere* but generally you can't see them, which is pretty handy 'cos they'd scare the pants off you if you *did*!

Angels are exceptionally good at **protecting** people who worship God – such as **Shadrach**, **Meshach** and **Abednego**. These guys were best mates with Daniel (of the lions' den) but *not* so pally with **King Nebuchadnezzar** of Babylon. They refused, point blank, to bow down and worship a statue of the king so he had them flung into a **sizzling hot furnace**. (It was *so* hot that the guards who threw them in got burned to a **crisp**!).

OH DEAR!
I CAN NEVER
GET THE
HANG OF
BARBECUES!

When the king peeked in (from a *good* distance) much to his surprise, there weren't three, but **four** men now in the furnace. **Daniel 3 verses 19** to **25** has the whole story and you can see where an angel features in all this.

ANGELS

If you think angels are just **wimpy creatures** with **curly gold hair** and **pretty wings** then it's time to think again. We'll dive straight into this Bible bit about **King David,** who's just done something he's *about* to **regret**. It might sound *trivial* but David had taken a **census** to find out how many men in Israel were available to fight in the army, if they were needed. (1,300,000 if you must know).

Why was it a mistake? 'Cos Israel wasn't supposed to rely on the *size* of its **army** but the *size* of its **God**! It was decision time for Israel's king.

Israel was going to be punished, but *David* was allowed to choose *how*.

He settled for the **three day epidemic**.

That's where the *angel* comes in.

The angel swept across the land putting to death the Israelites in their **thousands** until even *God* could stand it no more.

Precisely how *many* Israelites died can be seen in **2 Samuel 24, verse 15**.

ANGELS

What sort of person are you? Are you a fairly **predictable** type who *doesn't* like change? Do you *hate* it when your mates drop in unannounced and they catch you watching **toddler's TV**? Well, you're not alone. What we've got here in *this* story is a bunch of **shepherds** (middle eastern variety) just minding their own business, doing typical shepherd-like things such as looking after sheep (what else?) when, who should drop by, but an **angel**. To be honest the shepherds' reaction wasn't so much one of annoyance as ...

And so would yours have been if you were suddenly greeted by an angel from God in the dead of night. Angels were **awesome**! Being kind the angel told them *not* to be frightened, he'd only dropped by with a spot of **good news**. Phew! *There's* a relief! He'd come to tell them that **Jesus** (God's Son) had just been born nearby and if they wanted *proof* then it was that the baby would be wrapped in strips of cloth (as was the tradition) and lying in a manger (cattle trough).

Get yourself into a **Christmassy mood** by reading the *rest* of this Bible bit in the book of **Luke, chapter 2 verses 13** to **20**. In the process you'll also discover who *else* dropped by as the shepherds looked on (verse **13** is a clue!).

MURDER

A lot of people think that you've gotta be some sort of *saint* before God takes any sort of notice of you. That would rule **Moses** out for *starters*. You remember him, don't you? He's the one who sailed down the river Nile in a basket (as a baby) and ended up being adopted into Egypt's **royal family**. (Full story in Boring Bible book *Magnificent Moses*.) Moses wasn't actually an Egyptian at all – he was a **Hebrew** (or Israelite). And like *all* the Hebrews in Egypt, they were slaves – and **badly treated slaves** at that.

Moses **hated** to see the Hebrews (his own people) being overworked and ill-treated by the Egyptian slave masters. He felt **powerless**. Then one day, when Moses was a grown man, he witnessed an Egyptian **beating** one of his own people. Checking to see that nobody was looking, he killed the Egyptian there and then and buried him in the sand.

But was Moses safe or did he get found out?
Exodus chapter 2 verse 13 to **16** will give you the lowdown.

And *here's* the good part,
Despite Moses' crime, God *still* used him to free the Hebrews from slavery. Which means that God can use *anybody*!

KINDNESS

One guy who seems to crop up quite a *bit* in this book is **King David**. That's because when push came to shove he really only wanted to do what pleased God. Although David sometimes made **mistakes** he *also* did a lot of things **right**, which is *why* he pops up on *this* page.

Before David had been crowned king of Israel he'd been best buddies with King Saul's son, **Jonathan**. They really hit it off, even though Saul had it in for David. Now *David* was king, and he thought back to his friendship with Jonathan and decided to repay Jonathan's **kindness** to him. Jonathan was long dead. In fact descendants of Saul were few and far between. But when King David found out about Jonathan's crippled son (**Mephibosheth**) he had him brought to the palace. No doubt Mephibosheth was thinking that the king was about to take revenge on him because of his grandad's long-running feud with David. Nothing could be *further* from the truth.

David gave back to Mephibosheth *all* the land that had belonged to King Saul which made him **one rich Mephibosheth**! David didn't stop there.

He *also* said that Mephipbosheth would be treated just like one of his own sons...

NO, MEPHIBOSHETH, YOU CAN'T GO OUT UNTIL YOU'VE DONE YOUR HOMEWORK!

...and **2 Samuel chapter 9 verse 10** tells you what *other* act of kindness David bestowed on Jonathan's crippled son.

PROMISES

How many times have you said you'll do something, only to break your word? **Keeping promises** is a real **toughie**, isn't it? Even when you try your very *best* to keep one, sometimes you still fail through no fault of your own. **Abram** (later called Abraham) was feeling a bit sorry for himself. God had promised him **lots of good things** but Abram figured that it wouldn't be much use to him because when he died there would be no children to inherit the stuff. Good point!

So God led Abram outside and used the sky as the world's biggest visual aid.

He told Abram to look up at the night sky and **count the stars**. Have a go yourself, you'll soon find out that it's **impossible**. And even if you *could* count every single star that you could see just with your eyes there would still be all the **millions** of ones out there which you *couldn't* see.

LOOK AT THE SKY AND TRY TO COUNT THE STARS. YOU WILL HAVE AS MANY DESCENDANTS AS THAT

The Bible says that Abram **trusted God's promise** and God was **pleased** with him.

This Bible story appears in **Genesis chapter 15** from **verse 1** to **6**, but why not *also* check out **Exodus chapter 1 verse 7** to see what had become of Abram's decendants a few hundred years later.

You'll soon find out whether or not God's promises can be trusted.

BARBECUES

If you've just read the *previous* page then we're sticking with Abram (or should I say **Abraham** as he's *now* known) for *this* page as well. Just like God had promised, Abraham *did* have a family of his own and **Isaac** (his son) is about to head off with his dad for a bit of good ol' father and son time together.

But not *everything* was as it seemed. There was something *different* about *this* family outing. For a start, Abraham had packed a **donkey-load of wood**. What could *that* be for?

After a three days they arrived in the land of **Moriah**. Very pretty it was as well, especially the big mountain which they were planning to climb. Abraham stacked the pair of them up with bundles of **wood**, **coals** and a **knife** (a *knife*?!!) and off they set. (Hmm ... no packed lunch?).

At which point Isaac twigged what was going on. His dad was going to make a **sacrifice to God**. What a great idea. Just one problem. No animal to sacrifice. Then Isaac 'twigged' some more ...

DON'T ASK ME HOW I WORKED IT OUT – JUST CALL IT INTUITION!

He was going to be the sacrifice ... Abraham picked up the knife to kill his **only son** and ...

Don't let me be the one to spoil the ending. Look it up yourself in **Genesis chapter 22** and from **verses 11** to **14**.

BUILDINGS

How many men does it take to build a temple for God to live in? Don't worry, you don't need to work it out – the Bible gives us the **exact** number which is **183,300**.

How *long* it took is for *you* to find out at the end. This mammoth building project was originally the brainchild of **King David** but it was carried out by his son, **Solomon** (the *next* king of Israel).

Because God was planning to take up residence in the **Temple**, everything had to be the very *best*.

Cedar and **pine trees** were imported from **Lebanon** by being tied together and floated down the coast to Israel (just like modern day loggers do to transport their logs to the sawmills).

80,000 men were employed in the quarries cutting the stones for the Temple, but at the Temple site no hammer, axe or any other iron tool was used so that the noise level was kept to a **minimum**.

Everything was built according to precise instructions as given by God. It was going to be a **replica** of where God lived in heaven so it had to be **perfect**.

Absolutely *no* expense was spared. The whole inside of the Temple was covered in **gold**. Only the *best* for God.

So, how long did it take to build?

Look up **1 Kings chapter 6 verse 38**. But don't stop there. Read on into the next chapter to see what Solomon built *next*.

A NICE WOODEN GARDEN SHED, PERHAPS?

Er, no, not quite!

BUILDINGS

If you're impressed by pyramids then you'll be knocked sideways by a **ziggurat** (a huge temple tower). *This* Bible bit is early on in the history of planet earth and things are *still* getting back to normal after the world having been destroyed by a whopping great flood. Noah's descendants had been told (by God) to repopulate the earth once more, but as the people came to the flat plains of **Babylonia** they halted. They'd wasted no time in drifting away from God and choosing to do their **own thing** instead ...

COME ON! LET'S MAKE BRICKS AND BAKE THEM HARD. NOW LET'S BUILD A CITY WITH A TOWER THAT REACHES THE SKY SO THAT WE CAN MAKE A NAME FOR OURSELVES AND NOT BE SCATTERED ALL OVER THE EARTH.

Bad move, guys!

When God says go and repopulate the earth it's a good idea to do what he says... **or live with the consequences**.

Up until *that* time everybody spoke just the *one* language.

So what did God do to make *sure* they carried out his plan to fill the earth with people?

Well take a look at **Genesis chapter 11** and from **verse 5** through to **verse 9**.

MONEY

Have you noticed that if you ask *most* people what they would like if they had **three wishes**, there's a very good chance that having **loads of money** would be *one* of them. Everybody seems to want to be *rich*, which is no change (pardon the pun) from when *Jesus* was around.

I suppose that's why he spoke about **money** quite a lot. Jesus had worked out that money was often the very *thing* that *stopped* people making God **number one** in their lives.

But Jesus *also* knew that if they really, *really* loved him and wanted to serve him then they'd be **generous** people.

So, as far as God is concerned, how you treat your cash says a lot *about* you.

That's why the lady in *this* story is a bit of a star.

Jesus was hanging out in **God's Temple** (in Jerusalem) and was keeping his eye on the **money box** which collected donations for the upkeep of the building.

Most people were simply dropping in their **spare cash** which was sort of like giving God a **tip**. (Very insulting!).

I'LL NEED A RECEIPT FOR TAX PURPOSES!

But when a **poor widow** came onto the scene she put in her **entire worldly wealth**. She gave God **everything**. Now *that's* the sort of giving God likes!

The book of **Luke chapter 21** and **verse 2** will allow you access to her bank balance.

HEAVEN

What sort of thing are you expecting to read about in *this* Bible bit? Lots of people sitting on **fluffy white clouds** playing **harps**? Then you'd better think again, 'cos what you're about to read is gonna **blow your mind**.

Lots of people think that **heaven** is just a made-up sort of place but that's definitely *not* what the Bible says. In fact, you can't get *away* from stuff about heaven. Why? Easy! Heaven's where **God** lives. You're gonna need to read *this* Bible bit in full if you *really* want to get the full flavour of what's going on in heaven (at this very moment) but here's a little **taster**.

First off, at the very *centre* of things, on his throne, is **God**. Is he an old man with a beard? Check *that* one out for yourself.

Then there's twenty-four elders (important guys) sitting in a big circle around God and doing **24/7 non-stop worship**.

As for noise, well quiet it is *not*!

You've got **thunder** and **lightening** as special effects.

And as for the creatures surrounding God's awesome throne they need to be *seen* to be *believed*.

They've got eyes *everywhere*.

Go on, check it out in **Revelation chapter 4**.

HEAVEN

Who likes stories?
Yep, me too. That's why
Jesus used to do a lot of
his teaching using stories
(called parables). *One* of them was about a man named **Lazarus**
who'd been a **beggar** while he was alive, from which you've
probably worked out that he was now **dead** (clever clogs). But
don't worry about Lazarus *too* much, this story *does* have a
happy ending for him...

WELL IT CAN HARDLY GET ANY WORSE CAN IT?

Lazarus wasn't the *only* person in this story to have breathed his
last. We've also got a **rich man** centre stage, but *he* doesn't get
given a name, so we'll just have to call him '**the rich
man**'(inspired).

Lazarus hung out near to where the rich man lived, desperate
for any **scraps of food** he could get. This didn't seem to
concern the rich man in the *slightest*, which is probably one
good reason why he and Lazarus didn't end up in the same
place when they died. Lazarus made it to **heaven** but the rich
man ended up in a place called **hell**.

Things were *so* bad in hell that the rich man wanted to warn the
rest of his family about it, but as far as *God* was concerned he'd
already made it perfectly clear through the **Bible** and his
prophets that people need to get their lives sorted with God
before they die. So, how bad is hell?

Verses 22 to **24** of **Luke chapter 16** give a very clear picture.

SHIPWRECKS

Most of us would settle for just *one* shipwreck in our lifetime. But **Paul** (from the New Testament bit of the Bible) seemed to have a bit of a *thing* about them. He'd been shipwrecked **three times**! We meet up with Paul as he's on his way to see **Caesar** (the ruler of the Roman Empire). Paul wasn't actually guilty of *anything* but it's a long story and we haven't got time for it now. The long and the short of it was that he was being escorted along with a ship-full of *other* convicts across the **Mediterranean Sea**. Between you and me, autumn was not a *good* time to be making this voyage. The ship they were in was supposed to be edging its way round the coast of **Crete** to find a safe harbour for the winter.

ANY CHANCE OF AN UPGRADE TO FIRST CLASS?

Unfortunately, a strong wind blew up and cast the ship out onto the open seas. For **fourteen terrifying days** they were tossed about, fearing at every moment for their lives.

An **angel** appeared to Paul to reassure him that God would save them all – but the *ship* would be lost.

At long last the sailors caught sight of land.

Here's some questions for you to look into.

What was the land? How *many* people were on the ship?

How *many* days hadn't they eaten for?

Head for **Acts chapter 27 verse 33** and read right through to **chapter 28 verse 1**.

ATTACKS

This Bible story almost certainly takes the biscuit for *unusual* ways to conquer a city. Just to fill you in, the **Israelites** were in the process of clearing the land of **Canaan** of all its **wicked inhabitants** (mainly so as *they* could live there instead). First on the list was the walled city of **Jericho** ...

God's plan of attack was **highly unconventional** and probably wouldn't get in *any* army manual on '**How To Win Battles**'. This was the plan ...

With the **priests** blowing trumpets or carrying the ark of the covenant (a special box that represented God's presence with them) and accompanied by the entire **Israelite army**, they were simply to march *once* around the city, each day, for six days. Sounds perfectly straightforward to me.

On day **seven** they were to march round Jericho as before, but **seven times**.

With a single **blast** from the priests' trumpets and a **shout** from the army, guess what happened?

The Bible book of **Joshua chapter 6** and from **verse 20** onwards gives the *full* battle report.

WICKED WOMEN

When it comes to downright wickedness, **Jezebel**, the wife of the equally wicked **King Ahab** of Israel tops the charts. She'd make **Cruella De Vil** look positively *angelic*. To be honest, Ahab should *never* have married her in the *first* place. She wasn't even an Israelite, which meant she brought with her the worship of **Baal** (the evil god of her country). Not content with polluting Israel with her wicked religion, she set about having all of God's prophets **killed** and *replaced* with prophets of Baal.

As you can well imagine, God was not at *all* pleased.

In fact, through his prophet **Elijah**, he predicted Jezebel's violent death, which is the bit we're gonna dive right into now.

Jezebel's hubbie (Ahab) was dead and now her son **Joram** has just been assassinated by a guy called **Jehu**.

Now it's *Jezebel's* turn. The Bible tells us that she was doing her make-up when Jehu entered town.

Jezebel poked her head out of the window and started shouting insults. Jehu had had *enough* of Jezebel's evil antics and shouted back to some of the **palace officials** to throw Jezebel out of the window ...

I'D PREFER TO USE THE STAIRS IF THAT'S OKAY!

And throw her out they did.

I'd better warn you that it's a pretty **gory** ending, so you can decide if you're up to reading it or not.

It can be found in **2 Kings chapter 9** from **verse 30** to **37**.

Just make sure you read it on an *empty* stomach!

EARTHQUAKES

Paul and Silas, a couple of the world's first *ever* Christians, were on their travels telling people about Jesus and demonstrating with healings and miracles that he was very much **alive and kicking**. Not *everybody* liked what they were doing and the pair of them suddenly found themselves locked up in prison (in **Philippi**) on **trumped up charges**. *That* didn't seem to bother Paul and Silas too much.

The Bible says that at about midnight they were **praying** and **singing hymns** to God ...

Suddenly, a **violent earthquake** shook the prison to its foundations, all the **doors flew open** and the prisoners' **chains fell off**. The jailer woke up (which in the circumstances is no surprise) and thought that all his prisoners had escaped, which would have meant the **death penalty** for him.

Just as he was about to draw his sword and save his masters the effort, Paul stopped him and told him that *nobody* had escaped. What happened *next* was even *more* spectacular and can be found in **Acts chapter 16** and **verses 29** to **34**.

GRUB

How do you feed hundreds and hundreds and thousands of people in the middle of a **desert** when doorstep pizza deliveries haven't even been invented yet?

That's the problem **Moses** had when the whole **Israelite** nation had left their lives of slavery in Egypt and were making for the land of **Canaan**. They were getting a bit of a reputation for *grumbling*, and not having the world's best diet was cheesing them off something *rotten*. God had heard their moaning and was going to sort things out once and for all.

God appeared to the Israelites in all his **dazzling glory** to tell them what he was going to do.

Each evening they would have **meat** – and that *very* night a large flock of **quails** flew in and covered the camp. **Grub up!**

And each morning, when the dew had evaporated, the desert floor was covered with a thin and flaky substance – sort of like frost to look at. *This* was **breakfast**.

God gave them strict instructions on how *much* food to collect, and also a **special rule** for the Sabbath rest day.

You'll come across *that* bit in **Exodus chapter 16** and from **verse 22** to **36**.

And you'll *also* find out what this **flaky stuff** tasted like and *what* it was called.

HAS ANYONE GOT ANY KETCHUP?

GRUB

It makes a bit of a change to be told that **fruit** *isn't* good for you, doesn't it? But that's *exactly* what God told **Adam** and **Eve** way back at the dawn of time when they lived in the **Garden of Eden**.

Everything was brilliant and wonderful for the world's first two human beings – that was *until* they decided to **disobey God**. I suppose you *could* say it was a sort of test of how much they loved and respected the God who'd made them; out of everything in the garden there was just *one* solitary tree that they *weren't* allowed to eat the fruit from. To eat fruit from the tree that gave knowledge of good and evil was a **death sentence**. (It would make them like God – which was not on). Little did they know that God's enemy, the devil, in the guise of a **serpent** was about to trick them into doing the unthinkable ...

First *Eve* took a bite of the forbidden fruit and then *Adam*. The *unhappy* ending is all revealed in **Genesis chapter 3**. While you're at it, see if you can discover what **two sets** of clothing Adam and Eve wore.

NARROW ESCAPES

Here's a story that shows that God will only put up with wickedness for so long and then he calls time. Our main man in *this* story is a guy called **Lot** (which I suppose is better than being called **Less**). Lot was Abraham's **nephew** but they'd both settled down in different places. Lot had opted for **Sodom** (which was a bad move) because Sodom was a city full of wickedness (and so for that matter was its neighbour, Gomorrah). God told Abraham that he was going to **wipe out** these corrupt cities, but Abraham pleaded that if God could find just *ten* good people, would he spare them? God agreed and sent **two angels** down to do a spot of reconnaissance work. Their worst fears were confirmed, The place was the **height of wickedness**. Time was up for Sodom (and Gomorrah). The angels told Lot to take his family and evacuate the city or they'd be destroyed along *with* it. Nobody would believe Lot but he managed to get his wife and two daughters out just in the nick of time.

OH DEAR, I THINK I'VE LEFT THE LIGHTS ON!

How Sodom and Gomorrah were destroyed is detailed in **Genesis chapter 19** and from **verses 23** to **29**.
And can you *also* find out why Lot's wife *wasn't* a pillar of strength and what *sort* of pillar she turned out to be?

NARROW ESCAPES

I don't know about you but I *love* Christmas. But I'm afraid there's always a few **Scrooges** lurking in the wings, and **King Herod** of Israel was *one* of them.

He'd just had an unexpected visit from some **wise men**, who really made his **ears burn** with the news that a *new* king of the Jews (**Jesus**) had just been born in *his* land. He was well miffed! There was only room for *one* king and that (as far as *he* was concerned) was *him*.

He hastily called together all the religious leaders to see if they had any clues as to *where* this **Messiah** (as he was called) might have been born. No problem. The Bible told them with pin-point accuracy that **Bethlehem in Judah**

IT'S MY CROWN AND NOBODY ELSE IS GONNA PLAY WITH IT, OKAY?!

was the location to go looking for this **baby king**.

Herod tried to trick the wise men into coming back and telling him where the Messiah was living (once they'd paid their respects) but God warned them in a dream that this was *not* a good idea – so they returned a *different* way.

Herod soon realised that he'd been **out-smarted** and ordered that *every boy* in the Bethlehem region who was two or under must be **killed**.

How did *Jesus* escape this terrible slaughter?

Have a glance in Bible book **Matthew chapter 2** and **verses 13** to **15**.

SOLDIERS

One of the big *downsides* to being conquered is that everywhere you go there are **soldiers** hassling you. *Israel* had had its fair share of invading armies and the **Romans** were the very latest conquerors to take up residence ...

A LITTLE BIT OF TIME TO OURSELVES WOULD BE NICE, ONCE IN A WHILE!

But the Romans weren't *all* bad. In fact some of them seemed to take more of a shine to **Israel's God** than the *Jewish* people themselves. For instance, one day Jesus was just entering a small town called **Capernaum** when he was met by a **Roman officer**. The man's daughter was desperately unwell and the man *pleaded* with Jesus to heal her.

Now that wasn't unusual. People were *forever* asking Jesus to make them well. But what impressed Jesus about this military man was his complete and utter *confidence* that Jesus could do it with just a **word of command**.

The officer explained that he understood all about being **under authority** and *also* having his **orders obeyed**.

He could see that Jesus was under *God's* authority so that meant when he gave commands **things happened**.

The good news is that the girl got better that very *instant* but Jesus *also* said something very interesting about this Roman officer. To find out what it was, go to **Matthew chapter 8** and **verse 10**.

PLAGUES

If there's one *big* lesson the Bible teaches you it's this ...
Don't mess with God!

One person who was a bit *slow* on the uptake was **Pharaoh** (king of Egypt). He was holding the Israelite nation captive as **slaves**, so God sent a guy called **Moses** to tell the Pharaoh to release them ...

... which *wasn't* an encouraging start.

Time to implement **Plan B**.

God told Moses to tell Pharaoh that he was going to send a whole heap of **plagues** to persuade Pharaoh to change his mind.

And here they come...

1. All the water turned to **blood**. 2. **Frogs** everywhere. 3. **Gnats** everywhere. 4. **Flies** everywhere. 5. All the **animals** died. 6. Painful **boils** (ouch!). 7. **Hail** like you've never seen it before. 8. **Locusts** everywhere. 9. **Darkness** for three days. 10. The death of the **first-born**.

A quick investigation of **Exodus chapter 12** and **verses 29** to **42** will let you know whether Pharaoh was finally persuaded.

What's really *amazing* is that all the while the Egyptians were suffering these terrible plagues, not *one* of the Israelites was the least bit affected by them!

MAGICIANS

Surprised to see **magicians** in the Bible? Well don't be. Magicians were just people who chose to use the *Devil's* power instead of *God's*. That made them an **enemy of God** because *that's* what the Devil was.

Our story takes us to a Mediterranean island called **Paphos**. *That's* where **Paul** and **Barnabus** had arrived to tell the islanders that **Jesus** had made it possible for them to be forgiven for all their wicked ways.

Sergius Paulus (the governor of Paphos) was keen to meet this dynamic pair. Everywhere they went *miracles* from God seemed to happen, and Sergius Paulus wanted a **slice of the action.**

Not so **Elymas the magician**. He was dead against *everything* Paul and Barnabus stood for.

He did his level best to thwart them and spoil things.

But Elymas should have known better than to mess with Paul ...

YOU SON OF THE DEVIL! YOU ARE THE ENEMY OF EVERYTHING GOOD. YOU ARE FULL OF ALL KINDS OF EVIL TRICKS AND YOU ALWAYS KEEP TRYING TO TURN THE LORD'S TRUTHS INTO LIES! THE LORD'S HAND WILL COME DOWN ON YOU NOW. YOU WILL BE BLIND AND WILL NOT SEE THE LIGHT OF DAY FOR A TIME...

And it happened – just like Paul said.

What became of Sergius Paulus is revealed in **Acts chapter 13** and **verse 12**.

CHEATS

My dad always told me that cheats never prosper but **Jacob** seems to come out smiling in *this* Bible bit.

His dad (**Isaac**) is on his **death bed** but *before* he gives up the ghost he fancies something to eat. (Can't quite see why he'll be needing it but that's up to *him*). But it's not *Jacob* who gets to wear the chef's hat but his twin brother, *Esau*. Not only that, but Isaac is planning to round things off by giving Esau (the older of the two boys) his **blessing,** which was really important in those days.

Rebecca (the boys' mum) had a soft spot for Jacob and thought that *he* should be having the blessing instead, so she set about thinking up a cunning plan to make certain he jolly well *did*! While Esau was out hunting for something tasty to cook, Rebecca was getting Jacob dressed in **goats' skins** so that he felt **hairy** to the touch – just like his **hairy big brother**. (Isaac was almost blind so *he* wouldn't notice the difference).

Jacob (with his mum's help) sneakily served up freshly cooked goat with bread on the side. (Yummy!)

To cut a long story short, Isaac fell for the deception, hook line and sinker and *Jacob* got the blessing.

But he was found out (my dad was right after all!)

Read all about it in **Genesis chapter 27** from **verse 30** to verse **45**.

CHEATS

Not only does *Bible Buster* give over a whole **page** to the wicked Queen Jezebel, but her hubbie **Ahab** also has his very own page. Ahab was king of Israel but a pretty poor one – in fact, he was a right **sulky old so-and-so**. When a man called **Naboth** refused to sell him his **family vineyard** King Ahab went into a complete **strop**. He slumped on his bed and wouldn't eat *anything*.

That vineyard would have been *perfect* for the palace vegetable garden and now he couldn't have it. Not fair!

WELL I'M NOT LETTING NABOTH PLAY WITH MY GAMEBOY THEN!

Jezebel told Ahab to stop being such a **wimp**.
She'd get that vineyard – by hook or by crook (and a **crook** she most *definitely* was!).
Jezebel hatched an evil plan to stitch Naboth up good and proper by having him accused (falsely) of cursing God.
Guess what the punishment for that was? **Death**.
Naboth was stoned to death outside the city and Ahab went to take possession of the vineyard.
King Ahab hadn't bargained on *God* getting involved.
Through the prophet **Elijah**, God told Ahab that in the very place that Naboth had been killed, **dogs would lick up his blood**. (Yuk!).
Race to **1 Kings chapter 22** and **verses 37** and **38** to see if this came true.

CHASES

Jacob seemed to *specialise* in being on the run. *First* he was trying to escape from his brother Esau (after cheating on him) and *now* he was scarpering from his **Uncle Laban** who had played Jacob at his own game and cheated on *him* for a change. Jacob had worked his *socks* off for his uncle in exchange for marrying Laban's daughters, **Leah** and **Rachel**. It was time for Jacob to leave and head back to his own land. Jacob didn't want to return empty-handed. A good-sized flock of goats (like Laban had promised him) would *really* set him up for his new life. While Laban was out and about, Jacob took his family (and a good-sized flock of goats) and escaped Laban's clutches.

It took Laban **three whole days** to realise he'd been tricked. He was **mad**!

With his sons in tow, Laban set off in **hot pursuit** ...

It took him **seven days** to catch up with his runaway nephew, but just before that an **angel from God** warned Laban not to lay a *finger* on Jacob.

Did Laban and Jacob settle their differences?

Genesis chapter 31 and **verses 43** through to **55** has the answer.

STORIES JESUS TOLD

Okay, here's something *just* for all you **kids** out there. (Surprise, surprise, *some* **grown-ups** have actually been caught secretly reading Boring Bible books!)

Jesus made a big thing about kids because (unlike loads of grown-ups) they were prepared to take what he said at face value. Kids are usually far more **trusting**, which as far as *God* is concerned is a **good thing**. So, anybody who *stops* a child getting to know God is in **big trouble**.

Jesus told a story about some **sheep** to make it clear how *precious* kids are to God.

It was all about a **shepherd** who had **100 sheep** (no more, no less). Well not until *one* of them decided to wander off. Did the shepherd give up the sheep for lost and figure that he *still* had 99 left, or did he go and look for it?

Yep, you're right! He set off to find it.

Don't worry, this story has a happy ending.

The shepherd found the sheep and was **overjoyed**, which Jesus said was how **God in heaven** feels when a child returns to *his* family.

Look it up in **Matthew chapter 18** then run your finger down to **verse 10** to check out *who* kids have looking out for them.

STORIES JESUS TOLD

I'll bet there are days when you really wish you *didn't* have to go to **school**, aren't there? (And I'm *not* meaning you teachers who are taking sneaky look at this book.) The trouble is, if you don't *learn* anything then there won't be many jobs open to you when you finally leave school. And it's no good just *going* to school without taking a blind bit of notice of *what* the teachers are telling you. You'll get **nowhere fast** taking *that* route. **Jesus** was into teaching in a *big* way. There was stuff that people needed to know about God which would give them a **good start** in life, so loads of his time was spent **taking class** (usually out in the open air).

One *particular* lesson was all about a couple of guys who decided to have a go at **building a house**.

But there's more to building a house that cementing a few bricks together.

You've gotta build it *properly* or you'll come a **cropper** – just like one of *these* two men who built his house on **sand**. When a storm blew up, the house fell down. The other guy had a bit more sense and built *his* pad on **solid rock**.

So, what's the meaning of this handy bit of teaching?

A spot of swotting up is called for in **Matthew chapter 7 verses 26** and **27**.

STORIES JESUS TOLD

Some people think that you've gotta be really **good** before God will even give you a **second glance**. Which is weird 'cos that's *not* what the Bible says.

Jesus told a **parable** (a story with a special meaning) to make this clear. It was all about a **huge feast** that a man threw. He sent out invitations to all his closest friends and acquaintances, but instead of jumping at the chance of a slap-up meal with this great man they sent back their rather feeble **excuses**, one by one.

"I've bought a field and must go and look after it."

"I have bought five pairs of oxen and am on my way to try them out."

(I made that last one up myself.)

When the man's servant came back with the news that all these people had turned him down it's worth a look in Bible book **Luke chapter 14** from **verses 21** through to **24** to see *who* he invited in their place.

(The man who threw the feast was meant to be God and the people who turned him down were those who figured that they could quite happily live without God, thank you very much.)

STORIES JESUS TOLD

If Jesus had been born in the 21st century then *some* of the stories he told might have been very *different*. Take the story about the **sower**. Everybody *then* *understood* about sowing seeds to grow things but *nowadays* most of us get everything we need from the **supermarket**. *This* Bible bit would have really appealed to the crowd of people Jesus was talking to. (It was *such* a big crowd Jesus had to get into a boat so they could all see and hear him).

It featured a **farmer** who was out and about **sowing seed**. Scattering seed is pretty unpredictable and not *all* of it landed in the right place ...

HE'S JUST PLAIN CARELESS IF YOU ASK ME!

Some of it hit the target, but some it landed on the **path** and was scoffed by hungry birds.

Some of it landed on **rocky ground** but because the soil wasn't deep enough the feeble shoots that sprang up soon withered in the heat of the sun.

Some of the farmer's seed fell among the **thorn bushes**, but as it began to grow the weeds choked the living daylights out of it.

The seed that made it to **good soil** had a field day (literally). It produced a **mega crop**.

If you're a little bit confused what this story is all about then you're in good company. Jesus had to explain it to his disciples as well, as you'll see in **Matthew chapter 13** and **verse 18** to **23**.

THE DEVIL

God's enemy, the **Devil**, wasn't content just to spoil things between Adam and Eve and God (way back at the beginning of the world). Nope! When he saw **Jesus** come onto the scene to *undo* all the damage that *he'd* done he set about doing everything he in his power to *stop* him.

Jesus was about **30 years old** and was getting ready to take **Israel** by storm and bring the Israelites back into being being best buddies with God. But *first off* Jesus had to **prove himself**. The Holy Spirit (**God**) took Jesus out into the **desert** to face his enemy ...

This was gonna be a *really* important **test** to see if Jesus could win out against the Devil's attempts to make *him* turn against God (his Father in heaven).

After **40 days** without food Jesus was ready to face the Devil. But God's enemy *didn't* attack Jesus with weapons – he was far too devious for *that*. Instead he tried to persuade Jesus to turn the **stones** into **food** (he must have been starved), to have anything he wanted if he'd just **worship** the Devil and finally to jump off the **Temple roof** (and get some angels to save him) to prove he really *was* God's Son. **Nothing doing!** Jesus came back at the Devil with stuff from the Bible to tell him he was *well* out of order. Jesus won the test **hands down** and **Luke chapter 4 verse 14** lets on what its effect on Jesus *was*.

FLOODS

I couldn't have picked a better day to write about *this* Bible bit. It's been **tipping** it down outside but that's absolutely *nothing* compared with the **deluge** that hit the earth early in the history of the world. Things had gone slowly downhill from the time Adam and Eve had rebelled against God, and before long the world was *filled* with **wickedness**. God could stand it no more. (The Bible says that he was sorry he'd ever *made* the human race). There was nothing for it but to **obliterate** the whole lot of them from the face of the earth (with a flood). Being fair, God noticed that **Noah** wasn't like the rest – he was **good**. God would *spare* Noah (and his family). He instructed Noah to build the **world's biggest boat** and fill it with **animals** so the world could be repopulated when the flood had subsided. Can you imagine building a boat *that* big, miles from the sea? People must have thought he was **off his rocker**.

The Bible tells us that it took Noah **100 years** to build (and he was *already* 500 years old when he started!).

Just as God promised, the flood came and wiped every *trace* of wickedness away.

Here's a challenge. Read the story in **Genesis chapter 7** and see if you can find out how long the flood continued.

FIRES

Moses pops up quite a lot in the Boring Bible books. *That's* because God used him to do some **awesome** stuff. Moses' *first* big time meeting with God was very unconventional. After doing a runner from Egypt, our main man is living in the **desert** looking after his father-in-law's sheep and goats (which is a *long* way from living in the Egyptian royal household as an adopted son).

Suddenly an **angel** from God appeared to Moses in all his **blazing brilliance**. At first sight it looked like a **bush** was **on fire** but it strangely *wasn't* burning up.

Moses edged closer to see what was up ...

MOSES! DO NOT COME ANY CLOSER. TAKE OFF YOUR SANDALS BECAUSE YOU ARE STANDING ON HOLY GROUND. I AM THE GOD OF YOUR ANCESTORS...

The Bible says that Moses was so *frightened* he couldn't even *look*.

God told Moses that he was sending him *back* to Egypt to set the Israelite people free. God *also* gave Moses **two amazing signs** to *prove* that he would be with him and which you can read about in **Exodus chapter 4 verses 1** through to **9**.

STONINGS

Being a follower of Jesus has never, *ever* been for wimps. And there are some places you could *easily* end up getting arrested and killed for it. **Stephen** (the star of our story) was one such man. He was around at the same time as **Jesus**, but when Jesus went back up to heaven it was the likes of *Stephen* who were left to *continue* doing the stuff Jesus did. Like telling people that they could get themselves *right* with God (because Jesus had taken the punishment for all their nasty sin). Now to *most* people that sounds like a **pretty good deal**, but not to the religious leaders who were around at that time. They'd been **jealous of Jesus** and preferred to live their lives by following *bucket loads* of petty rules and regulations ...

People like Stephen *really* got under their skin, so they arrested him and put him on trial. Stephen gave them a detailed history lesson about God and Israel... **and Jesus**. That was the **final** straw.

Want to see how **seethingly angry** they were then? Check out **Acts chapter 7 verses 54** to **60**.

STORMS

A *lot* of Jesus's time was spent travelling around and sometimes the *quickest* route was by **boat.** As usual, it had been a busy day for Jesus. but before nightfall he made the decision to head for the *other* side of the **lake**. Everyone piled into a boat and they pushed off from shore. You might think that sailing across a lake was a **doddle** but *this* lake was **huge** and it wasn't unusual for boats to be caught in **terrible storms**. Like the one that *suddenly* came upon Jesus and his disciples. The wind blew up and the waves began to spill over into the boat so that it was about to **fill with water**.
But then they did have *Jesus*, the Son of God, on board so perhaps they weren't *too* concerned about their predicament ...

On *second* thoughts ...
The disciples were **scared stiff** and they quickly roused Jesus (he'd been asleep!). Was *Jesus* frightened? No way! He just got to his feet and did what only someone with **God's authority** could do.
And you can find out precisely what that was in **Mark chapter 4 verse 39**.

WISE SAYINGS

King Solomon learned a very important lesson early on in his career of being a ruler and it was *this*. If you want to **succeed** then you've gotta get **wise.** Why? So that you can make **good decisions**. How do you *get* wise? Easy – ask *God* for wisdom (which is just what Solomon did). There's a whole Bible book crammed *full* of **wise stuff** that Solomon said and we've picked out a few gems for you to enjoy. Just for your info, the Bible calls these wise sayings '**Proverbs**'.

'Never get a lazy man to do something for you. He will be as irritating as vinegar in your teeth or smoke in your eyes.'

'The start of an argument is like the first break in a dam. Stop it before it goes any further.'

'Gossip is so tasty – we love to swallow it.'

'A stupid son can bring his father to ruin. A nagging wife is like water going drip-drip-drip.'

SORRY SIR, I ONLY FIX TAPS!

And last but not least, here's a proverb I want you to finish off by looking it up in **Proverbs chapter 29 verse 15**.

'Correction and discipline are good for children. If a child has his own way ...'

LETTERS

How would *you* feel if your **personal mail** ended up in a book for every Tom, Dick and Harry to see? Well, *that's* what happened to a guy called **Paul**. If he'd been alive *today* he'd have been forever **texting** or **e-mailing** anybody and *everybody*. But Paul didn't mind people taking a peek at his letters – that's why he'd *written* them in the first place. Paul's letters were meant to help people be better followers of Jesus. One of his extra long ones was to a church in a place called **Corinth** which is here ...

And here's a snippet of that letter ...

'Love is patient and kind. It is not jealous or conceited or proud. Love is not ill-mannered or selfish or irritable. Love does not keep a record of wrongs. Love is not happy with evil but is happy with the truth. Love never gives up.'

You can look the *whole* of this letter in Bible book **1 Corinthians** but this bit is in **chapter 13**.

LETTERS

If you like **mysteries** then *this* page is for *you*! Nobody knows who actually *wrote* the Bible book 'Hebrews' but it contains some *brilliant* stuff written to a bunch of **Jews** who'd become **Christians**, and was the writer's attempt to put them *straight* on a few things.

One of the things he wanted them to grasp was that they could trust Jesus **100%** and to *prove* it he rattled off a whole *list* of people who'd done just *that*.

It's like a Bible heroes' **Hall of fame**. Take a look at a bit of it ...

I KNOW WHO WROTE IT!

'To have faith is to be sure of what you hope for, to be certain of things you cannot see ... It was faith that made Noah hear God's warning about things in the future that he could not see ... It was faith that made Abraham able to become a father even though he was old and Sarah could not have children. He trusted God to keep his promise.'

Head off to **Hebrews chapter 11** and skip to **verse 30** to see *what* it was that made the walls of Jericho fall down.

POWER SHOWER

Have you checked out the page in this book where Jesus has a head to head with the Devil and Jesus comes out on top and then is *filled* with **God's power** to set him up for the job he'd come to earth to do? If you *have*, then this *next* Bible bit is along the same lines. The only *difference* is that Jesus has gone back to heaven and his disciples have been told to hang around in **Jerusalem** until Jesus sends them something they're gonna *need* if they want to carry on working for him.

THE SUSPENSE IS KILLING ME! YOU DON'T THINK IT'S SOMETHING LIKE A NICE SMART UNIFORM, DO YOU?

So, we've got a whole *house-full* of **believers** (Christians) biding their time wondering *what* Jesus had lined up for them.
And then the big day arrived (to coincide with the Jewish festival of **Pentecost**). Without warning a **loud noise** hit their ears, followed by a **strong wind** which blew a gale through the house. What happened *next* was even *more* awesome. It looked like fire was coming down from the sky, and as it did, the **tongues of fire** touched their heads. It was **God's power** (the power of the Holy Spirit) coming to fill them up so they could continue Jesus's work on earth. Jesus had been as good as his word.
The Holy Spirit enabled *each* of them to do something quite **amazing** which you can hunt out in **Acts chapter 2** and from **verse 4** through to **verse 12**.

ADVERTS

What, **adverts** in the *Bible*? How absolutely **terrible**! Whatever will they think of *next*? Well, before you get *too* hot under the collar, let me fill you in. Yes, there *are* adverts in the Bible but they're actually called **prophecies**. (What a let down – bet you were hoping to see **skateboards for sale** weren't you?) In fact there are *loads* of these adverts all *over* the Bible but a lot of them (over **300**) are adverts for just one *particular* person – **Jesus**.

Did you know that even *before* Jesus had been *born* God had told the world that Jesus was on the way and had given loads of *extra* detailed info so people wouldn't miss it when he arrived.

Here's a *handful* of these adverts ...

Remember the Christmas story and how Jesus's mum was Mary (the **virgin**)?

'THE VIRGIN WILL BE WITH CHILD AND WILL GIVE BIRTH TO A SON AND WILL CALL HIM IMMANUEL'
(WHICH MEANS GOD WITH US)
Isaiah chapter 7 verse 14

If you know your Bible just a *bit* you'll know that Jesus was born in **Bethlehem** (it even features in a Christmas carol – 'O Little Town of Bethlehem')

'BUT YOU BETHLEHEM... OUT OF YOU WILL COME...ONE WHO WILL BE RULER OF ISRAEL'
Micah chapter 5 verse 2

'SEE YOUR KING COMES TO YOU..RIDING ON A DONKEY...'
Zechariah chapter 9 verse 9

Look up this *last* advert in **John chapter 12** verses **12** to **15**.

PRISONERS

It's *one* thing being flung into **jail** for a crime that you've commited but a completely *different* matter when you're totally **innocent**. **Joseph** (the guy with the coloured coat) was one such man. After ending up in Egypt as a slave (with a helping hand from his conniving brothers) he'd risen through the ranks to become the personal servant of **Potiphar** (the captain of the palace guard). According to the *Bible*, our Joseph was a bit of a **hunk** which is why **Potiphar's wife** had her sights set on him. A bit of hanky panky with Joseph was top of her '**to do**' list but Joseph was an **honourable** sort of chap who **feared God** and turned down her advances (on more than one occasion).

One time, when Joseph tried to run from her (rather than betray his master) she grabbed his coat and pretended that she'd taken it after Joseph had tried to have his way with her. What *lies*! Our hero was well and truly **stitched up**.

He was thrown into prison ...

OUCH! I DON'T THINK THAT WAS MEANT TO BE TAKEN LITERALLY!

... where he stayed for **many years**.

The *upside* to this was that because Joseph managed to interpret Pharaoh's dreams things turned out *not* so bad in the long run – as can be discovered in **Genesis chapter 41** and from **verse 38** to **49**.

PRISONERS

Being chucked into jail must be the *pits* but **Jeremiah** had to endure something worse – the **pit** itself! Jeremiah was a **prophet of God** but things were *not* looking rosy for God's people (the Jews). They were worshipping **idols** and living **wicked lives** and God was about to punish them for it. The whole nation was about to be attacked and conquered by the **Babylonians** and *that* was the end of it. Guess who he sent to tell them the bad news? Yep, *Jeremiah*. Let's just say that they didn't take what he had to say too well. Their army was *already* beginning to get all **anxious** about the Babylonians and the *last* thing they needed was Jeremiah coming along and making them feel worse. So they flung him in a deep pit (a **well**, actually) but fortunately for Jeremiah it was empty (with the exception of a **carpet of sludgy mud**).

I'D PREFER A CARPET OF CARPET!

If it hadn't been for good old **Ebedmeleh** then Jeremiah would have starved to death down there but with the help of a bit of ingenuity from Ebedmelech, Jeremiah lived to prophecy another day, as you can check out in Bible book **Jeremiah chapter 38 verses 10** to **13**.

FRIENDS

What would *you* do if your dad was trying to kill your best friend? Now, that's probably a *ridiculous* question to ask, but *not* for **David** and **Jonathan**. God had already lined David up to be Israel's *next* king but **King Saul** (the *present* ruler) hated *everything* about him.

I WOULDN'T SAY THAT! THOSE SANDALS HE'S WEARING AREN'T TOO BAD!

Jonathan (Saul's son) had a bit more of a **soft spot** for young David and did his best to keep the peace, particularly as David was living under the *same roof* as King Saul.

Things were coming to a head and David realised that if he didn't do something *soon* he'd end up **dead**.

He decided to test the waters by disappearing off the scene for a day or two to see what Saul's reaction was.

Jonathan was acting as middle man and was prepared to stick his neck out for his **best buddy**, David.

If Jonathan's dad got *uppity* about David's absence, then that that would be the *sign* that Saul wanted to kill David.

In fact, Saul was *more* than just 'uppity', he was **furious** and accused Jonathan of being **unfaithful** to him. With David not around, Saul flung his spear at his son *instead* (but missed – phew!)

Have a quick read of **1 Samuel chapter 20 verses 41** and **42** to see the best buddy's tearful parting (sniffle! sniffle!).

ENEMIES

Our story *begins* with a chappie called **Nehemiah** getting permission from the **Emperor of Persia** to go back to his homeland of **Israel** so he could set about rebuilding the city of **Jerusalem**. The walled city had been all but *destroyed* by its attackers and Nehemiah and his fellow countrymen had been carted off as slaves. *Amazingly*, Artaxerxes (the emperor) *agreed* to Nehemiah's request and *even* provided the **building materials** as an added bonus. Nehemiah figured (correctly) that *God* was behind all of this. But all was *not* plain sailing. As soon as Nehemiah set to work, a couple of wise guys called **Sanballat** and **Tobiah** began to heckle them ...

That made Nehemiah even *more* determined to rebuild Jerusalem's walls. Sanballat and Tobiah (together with a whole bunch of other cronies) decided to *really* **put the boot in** and attack Jerusalem.

So, Nehemiah set guards all around the city and even *those* who were carrying building materials worked **one-handed** (with a weapon in the other!).

How long did it take to **rebuild** the walls of Jerusalem? Probably *not* as long as you think.

Nehemiah chapter 6 verse 15 is where you need to be heading to find out.

SLIPPERY SNAKES

When God wanted to free the Israelite nation from slavery in Egypt you'd have thought he'd use something a bit more dramatic than **a stuttering man**, **his brother** and a **wooden stick**. But then *again*, God has always been more than a little bit **unconventional**. *That* way it's obvious that *he's* the one doing the amazing things – not *people*. Moses and his brother Aaron were about to have a head to head with **Pharaoh**, king of Egypt. Moses wasn't *too* clever with public speaking so Aaron was going to be his **mouthpiece**. So, *what* was the wooden stick for? Let's see.

Moses (through Aaron) told Pharaoh that he must free the Israelite people from their life of slavery in Egypt.

Pharaoh wasn't too impressed so Aaron threw his wooden stick down and before their very eyes it turned into a **slithering snake**. Stubborn Pharaoh wasn't going to be outdone and commanded his **magicians** to do the same thing – which they did. But God got the last laugh 'cos Aaron's snake gobbled up the *lot* of them.

Aaron's stick (or **staff,** as it was known) was used more than once, but have a read of **Exodus chapter 14** and **verse 15** onward to find out about its most *miraculous* use.

SLIPPERY SNAKES

This Bible bit follows on from the '**shipwreck**' one that we've already featured. The star of that story, **Paul**, is now safely ashore on the island of **Malta**. The islanders were *more* than welcoming, which is a lot more than you could say for the *weather*. It was **wet**, **cold** and **horrible**. Hardly the *best* weather for all those dripping wet castaways to get themselves dried out. As I hinted, the Maltese people were a friendly bunch and they soon had a **blazing fire** crackling away.

Paul couldn't seem to sit still for five minutes and the Bible says he'd gathered up a bundle of sticks for the fire *himself*.

Not *everyone* on the island had such a warm welcome for Paul, 'cos when he went to chuck the sticks onto the fire a **snake** jumped out (disturbed by the heat – and wouldn't *you* be?) and locked its **sharp teeth** into Paul's hand.

When the islanders saw Paul's predicament they put two and two together (*wrongly*) and concluded that Paul must have been a **murderer** and he was *now* getting his come-uppance.

But Paul simply shook the snake off and carried on. When Paul *didn't* drop down dead they *then* concluded that he must be a **god** instead. (Wrong *again!*)

WELL HOW ABOUT AN OPTICIAN...YOU LOOK LIKE ONE...OR WHAT ABOUT A ZOOKEEPER OR MAYBE A PIANO TUNER? TELL US WHEN WE'RE GETTING WARM!

As it happened Paul stayed on Malta for three months and you can find out *how* he passed the time in **Acts chapter 28** from **verse 7** through to **verse 10**.

BLOODY BATTLES

The Bible seems to feature its fair share of **family feuds** and no *more* so than that between **King David** and one of his sons, **Absalom**. Even though they'd fallen out David couldn't help loving his son and in his heart of hearts he wanted to be reconciled. But it *wasn't* to be and it got to the point where David and Absalom were at war with each other. The armies of Absalom and David met for a **final showdown**. It was now *all* or *nothing*.

David pleaded with his commanders *not* to harm his wayward son.

Split into units of a thousand, King David's men swept across the countryside, slaughtering the enemy in the **forest of Ephraim**. The Bible says that it was a terrible defeat with **20,000** men killed on that *one* day.

But *more* tragic was the how *Absalom* met his end ...

YOU CAN'T BEAT TRAVELLING BY MULE FOR A SAFETY

While riding his mule he stumbled across some of David's men and as the mule went under a **large oak tree** Absalom's **head** got caught in the branches. The mule ran off and Absalom was left **dangling helplessly in mid-air**.

Against David's orders, one of his commanders (**Joab**) plunged **three spears** into Absalom's chest, killing him (as I'm sure you'd worked out).

King David was never really the same again after that day and *nor* were things between him and Joab, which you can see by looking up **2 Samuel chapter 19** and **verses 1 to 8**.

SPIES

Okay, the story so far is that the **Israelite** nation had escaped from slavery in Egypt (with Moses as their leader) and were now on the *verge* of entering **Canaan** (the land that God had *given* them to live in). Time to do a spot of reconnaissance. Moses handpicked one leader from *each* of Israel's twelve tribes and sent them into Canaan as **spies** to see what the place was like ...

YOUR MISSION IS TO FIND OUT WHAT IT'S LIKE, HOW MANY PEOPLE LIVE THERE, HOW STRONG THEY ARE, IS THE LAND GOOD OR BAD, ARE THE TOWNS AND CITIES FORTIFIED, IS THE SOIL FERTILE AND LASTLY, IS THE LAND WOODED? OFF YOU GO MEN!

After **40 days** spying out the land the twelve men returned – **mission accomplished!**

They'd come back with a nice selection of Canaan's finest **fruit** to give Moses some sort of an idea how **lush** the place was, but they'd *also* come back with some **scary reports of giants** living in the land.

The upshot of this scaremongering was that the Israelites wanted to turn round and go *back* to Egypt.

Caleb and **Joshua** were the only two spies *not* to be frightened. *They* wanted to go in and take the land that God had promised to them. But that *didn't* happen. *Instead*, here's how God punished the Israelites' **disobedience**. Read **Numbers chapter 14 verses 29** and **30**, and also **verses 36** and **38** in the same chapter.

WET STUFF

The next couple of pages are most definitely *not* recommended reading for **cats** who as we all know have a thing about water (and not a *good* thing). We're going to whiz back to the **beginning of the world** (just as planet earth is being made) to see how it all came together.

The Bible's got quite a *bit* of info about what God used to pull it all together, and one of the *main* ingredients was good old **water**.

In fact, the earth was little more than a **raging ocean**, but if you'd been there (which you *couldn't* because people hadn't yet come onto the scene) you wouldn't have *seen* very much. It was **pitch dark**. Fortunately, the **next** thing God made was **light**, so we can now see where we're going.

THAT'S BETTER! I'M SCARED OF THE DARK!

Now for the *interesting* bit.

The Bible tells us that God separated the water into **two places** – *on* the earth and *above* the earth (probably a sort of protective water vapour canopy – check out Boring Bible book *Ballistic Beginnings*). *Next*, God pulled all the water on the face of the earth into *one* place so that land appeared – **just like that!**).

God called the water '**Sea**' and in **Genesis chapter 1 verses 20** to **22** you can see *what* he filled the sea *with*. And a quick shuffle along to **Genesis chapter 2 verses 5** and **6** will let you in on *how* God watered the plants and stuff. (*Very* ingenious I can tell you.)

WET STUFF

We *all* know that **camels** are capable of storing emergency supplies of water around in their **humps** but what about human beings? The **Israelites** were heading towards Canaan (the land that God had given them to live in) but all this walking was **thirsty work** and there weren't *too* many drinks dispensers out in the wilds. The Israelites started to **grumble** to **Moses** (their leader) about how hard done by they were ...

I'VE REALLY GOT THE HUMP – OR AT LEAST I WISH I DID!

They were all for *stoning* poor Moses, so he prayed to God and God told him to take his special **wooden stick** (or staff) and go the **Mount Sinai**. God would show Moses *which* rock to hit with the stick – which Moses did!

Result number one: Water poured out of the rock.

Result number two: God was displeased with the Israelites for constantly complaining and testing his patience by refusing to trust that *he* would take care of all their needs.

The place where the water sprung out of the rock was given **two** names which mean '**testing**' and '**complaining**'.

You can find out what they are in Bible book **Exodus chapter 17** and **verse 7**.

(And *no* complaining, okay!)

GARDENING

You'd have *thought* that the **first man** to live on planet earth would have the *pick* of the **jobs**. I mean, there'd hardly be any competition, now, *would* there? And you wouldn't *necessarily* need to do the **same** job two days running. You could take your pick. You could be a **king** on Monday, a **pop star** on Tuesday, a **scientist** on Wednesday, an **explorer** on Thursday and then maybe take Friday, Saturday and Sunday off as a long weekend. But guess what job the world's first human being got handed to do by God? **Gardener**! Stop laughing, I'm serious. Yep, our **Adam** was put in charge of all things **horticultural**.

LOOKS LIKE I WON'T BE NEEDING THESE THEN!

Actually, it's not *quite* so weird as it sounds, 'cos when God made Adam (and Eve) he *also* gave them somewhere wonderful to live called the **Garden of Eden**. It was the *best* garden you've *ever* seen and it was watered by a stream running right through it. Like all gardens it needed looking after, but God wanted *Adam* to have a bit of a say as to how things should look. God had made people **creative**, so Adam's ideas about how Eden should look were appreciated by God.

Adam and Eve eventually turned against God but I wonder if Adam still kept his job as head gardener?

Forage around in **Genesis chapter 3** and from **verse 22** to **24** for the answer.

KIDS

Do ever get made to feel that you're **in the way**? (Adults, please ignore this question – this is a *kids'* book so it's *kids* I'm talking to!) If the answer's '**yes**' then you've got a lot in common with the kids featured in this *next* Bible bit. In fact, right through the centuries kids have *often* been treated by *some* grown-ups as **second class citizens**. If you'd been around 150 years ago it was a case of kids were *seen* and *not heard* and could only speak when they were spoken to.

That sort of attitude to kids was around a bit in Jesus's time. One day, while **Jesus** was in the middle of a spot of his brilliant teaching, some people turned up at the house he was in – **with their kids**!

They'd seen how Jesus made sick people well and gave evil spirits their marching orders so they were keen to get Jesus to **bless their children**.

Just one small **problem**.

Jesus's **disciples**.

As far as *they* were concerned Jesus was *far* too busy to be bothered by laying hands on little kids ...

Big mistake!

Jesus was pretty angry with the disciples and **Mark chapter 10** from **verse 14** to **verse 16** will let you in on what *he* had to say on the matter.

GRUESOME DEATHS

Getting a message from God isn't *always* as pleasant as you might think.

King Eglon of Moab could *certainly* vouch for *that*! As per usual, the **Israelites** had been going through a phase of sinning against **God** and God punished them by allowing tubby King Eglon to conquer and rule them. As per usual, they *eventually* came to their senses, turned from their wicked ways and cried out to God to free them. Being **compassionate** and **forgiving**, God answered their prayers by sending **Ehud** to lead them. The Bible tells us that Ehud was a *left-handed* man (which, as you will soon see, was *very* important). Loaded down with a nice slection of **gifts** to sweeten Eglon up, Ehud paid a visit to the Ammonite king. But this wasn't the *only* reason for Ehud's courtesy call ...

YOUR MAJESTY, I HAVE A SECRET MESSAGE FOR YOU!

Crafty Eglon had secretly hidden a **50 centimetre sword** under his clothes. King Eglon wouldn't have been expecting danger from Ehud's *left* hand because swords were usually held *right-handed*. But Ehud broke with convention and plunged the sword into fat King Eglon's whopping great belly.

What became of the sword is waiting for you in **Judges chapter 3** and from **verse 21** through to **verse 25**. (Just make sure you're not eating your lunch as you check it out – you have been warned!

GRUESOME DEATHS

What would *you* want if I said you could have **anything** you asked for? Probably *not* what the **young girl** in our story requested. She was the daughter of **Herodias**, who'd been married to a guy called **Philip**, but was *now* married to **Herod**, the ruler of Galilee and (just to complicate things) Philip's *brother*. Are you still with me? Good!

John the Baptist (Jesus's cousin) had been given the job (by God) of getting everybody ready for Jesus coming onto the scene.

Herod had taken exception to John speaking out against his marriage to his brother's wife. So, he had John **locked up** ...

Herod was looking for a chance to get his own back on John and the opportunity came on his **birthday**.

He'd thrown a **slap-up feast** for all and sundry and things were going well.

Time for Herodias's daughter to do her party piece by **dancing** in front of her step-dad (Herod). He was *so pleased* that he swore to her she could have *anything* she asked for.

If you want to see *what* that was then a quick scan of **Matthew chapter 14** and **verse 8** to **12** will tell *all*.

MIRACLES

If you've heard about the story of Moses leading the whole Israelite nation through the middle of the Red Sea then *this* miraculous Bible bit won't surprise you at all. Just to set the scene, the **Israelites** were getting themselves geared up for conquering the land of **Canaan** (which was where they were planning to settle down). There was just one *teensy* problem – the **River Jordan** was blocking their way ...

No worries. God had *that* one sorted. He gave **Joshua** (their leader) strict instructions on what he wanted the Israelites to do at the given time. The **priests** were to carry the **Covenant Box** (which represented God's presence with them) as they waded into the River Jordan. This could be **dangerous** because the river was in flood. (The Bible tells us that it was harvest time, if you're *really* interested). With the Israelites following, the priests obeyed God's instructions to the letter. As soon as they set foot in the Jordan a **pathway** started to clear **before their very eyes**.

How it actually happened can be read in **Joshua chapter 3** and from **verse 14** to **verse 17**.

One thing's for sure – *that* miracle made the people of Canaan **scared silly** of the Israelites. With God on their side they were **invincible**!

MIRACLES

Elijah was a prophet-and-a-half by *all* accounts. He was getting some **big-time hassle** from King Ahab and Ahab's wife (Jezebel) so he decreed that there wouldn't be any **rain** (*or* dew) for the next **two or three years** (until *he* said so!).

Elijah then did what any right-minded person would have done in the circumstances and did a runner, as far from Ahab and Jezebel's seething clutches as possible. For a while, Elijah got fed and watered by some helpul **ravens** ... and a **brook**. When the brook had dried up (no rain!) God told Elijah go to **Zarephath** where a **widow** would take over the job of feeding him ...

Just as Elijah was entering the town, he met the lady concerned. She was gathering firewood to to cook up **one last meal** for herself and her son, then that was it for their food supply.
Hmm, *that* doesn't sound too good.
Elijah wasn't daunted though. *He* trusted God **100%**.
Elijah told the widow to bring her *last* **handful of flour** and her *last* **drop of olive oil** to prepare a meal. He promised that the bowl of flour and the jar of oil wouldn't run out until God sent rain again.
But was Elijah right?
1 Kings chapter 17 verse 15 and **16** will reveal the truth!

MIRACLES

We're heading *straight* to the Bible book of **Acts** (it's called that 'cos it's jam-packed *full* of **action**) to catch up on what's been happening with some of the world's first *ever* Christians. **God's power** seems to be *everywhere*, which means that the *unexpected* can be *expected* at any moment (if you get my drift). It was three o'clock in the afternoon and **Peter** and **John** (two Christians) were visiting **Jerusalem's Temple**. Before they had a chance to go any further Peter and John were confronted by a **lame beggar** *desperate* for money. The Jewish people were supposed to give money to poor people as part of their religion, so this lame man knew that hanging around the Temple was a **good move**! The Temple was **the** place as far as the Jewish religion was concerned, so you could *always* expect a good crowd to beg from.

The poor beggar must have been surprised when Peter looked *straight* at him and said ...

Did he accept Peter's gift?
Check it out in **Acts chapter 3 verses 7** through to **10**.

MIRACLES

God didn't just restrict his miracles to the *Israelite* nation. If someone was prepared to be humble before him then God was *always* willing to prove that he was a **loving** and **caring God**. Which brings us neatly to **Naaman**, Naaman was a seriously important guy in the **Syrian army** (a commander, in fact). The *bad news* was that Naaman suffered from a **terrible skin disease**. But the *good news* was that someone had told him that there was a prophet in Samaria (**Elisha**) who could cure him. The King of Syria dispatched Naaman off to see the prophet (with a sizeable amount of cash to pay him for his services – but which Elisha refused).
When Elisha told Naaman that he must **take a bath** in the **River Jordan** (seven times) the Syrian was *well miffed*.

ARE YOU SAYING THAT I SMELL?

He'd been expecting some sort of magic wand hocus-pocus and an instant cure. Naaman got really hot under the collar and was dead against washing in the dirty Jordan.
Fortunately, his servants managed to persuade their master, Naaman to change his mind. *Why* take a bath in a muddy river? Could it be that God wanted to test Naaman's obedience and humility? Whatever the reason, **2 Kings chapter 5** and **verses 14** and **15** is where you'll find out whether Naaman took his servants' advice.

MIRACLES

It's *one* thing seeing someone miraculously **healed** of something but *another* seeing someone **come back to life** after being **dead** a few days. Well, that's *exactly* what we've got here. The dead man in question was a guy called **Lazarus**. Jesus was well aware that Lazarus (a good friend) was ill but although Jesus was just across town he did *nothing* to heal him. All *Jesus* would say was that **God** would get the **glory** in the end. *Very* mysterious!

By the time Jesus arrived at Lazarus's house he'd been in the tomb for **four days** and Lazarus's sisters (Martha and Mary) were *distraught*.

The Bible says that Jesus was **deeply moved** by everything that had happened but *now* was the time for action.

Jesus ordered that the tomb stone be rolled away *despite* protests that the **smell** would be *awful*.

Jesus prayed to his Father in heaven and then called out in a loud voice ...

Can a dead man hear Jesus speaking to him?
Look it up in Bible book **John chapter 11 verse 44**.

MIRACLES

If you wanna see how **desperate** *some* people were to get to **Jesus** in order to experience a **miracle** then check out *this* story. We're in a place called **Capernaum** and just about the *whole* town seemed to have turned out to see Jesus and to hear what he had to say. Jesus was holding an *indoor* teaching meeting and the house was **busting at the seams**. When four guys turned up carrying their sick friend, their way to Jesus was barred by the large crowd.

Using their initiative, they made their way up to the roof (with their sick friend) and started to **pull the roof apart**.

I suppose they *could* have just turned around and gone back home having at least *tried* to get their friend to Jesus – but **no!** The small matter of a huge crowd and a roof weren't going to deter *them*.

They were **desperate** for a **miracle** and there was absolutely **no way** that they'd settle for second best.

With a **hole** cleared in the roof, the men lowered the paralysed man down – right in **front of Jesus**.

The *Bible* says that Jesus immediately saw that they had **faith** enough for a **miracle** and you can see what a result *this* brought about by reading the rest of the story in **Mark chapter 2** and from **verse 5** to **verse 12**.

THIEVES

It's *one* thing to rob *people* but *another* thing to steal from **God**. But *that's* what the people in *this* Bible bit are accused of. You're probably wondering how on earth *anyone* can nick *anything* from God. I mean, you can hardly sneak up to heaven while nobody's looking! Well you'd be right.

What we're looking at *here* is something called '**tithes**'.

The action takes place a few hundred years *before* Jesus is born and God's special nation (**the Israelites**) have had their magnificent **Temple** rebuilt and are trying to get things back to normal (after the small matter of the odd exile or two).

The trouble was that the Israelites *weren't* worshipping God *properly* – in fact, they weren't really taking their worship seriously at all. So God sent a prophet (**Malachi**) to tell them that they were being **lazy** and **corrupt** and to get their act together – **pronto!**

And *another* thing! The Israelites were *supposed* to give a '**tithe**' (10%) of their earnings to God for the upkeep of the Temple, but they *weren't*. The people were **short-changing God** and hoping he wouldn't notice. Not a good idea!

ONE FOR ME,
NONE FOR GOD.
ONE FOR ME,
NONE FOR GOD...

God's view was that by giving the **first tenth** of their dosh to God it showed that they put **him** first.

And a quick flick to **Malachi chapter 3 verses 8** through to **12** will let you see what God had to say on the matter.

BOATS

Moses must be in the running (or should I say 'sailing'?) for the title of **World's Youngest Sailor**.

At the tender age of **three months** he sailed *single-handed* up the **River Nile** (or at least *part* of it). *Why* and *how* I will now tell you. To give a quick bit of background, what we've got here is the Israelite nation living as slaves in Egypt. (If you want the *full* story then you're gonna have to fork out for a copy of Boring Bible book *Magnificent Moses* – sorry!)

Egypt's cruel **Pharaoh** was more than a little bit worried about the size of the Israelite population (and his ability to control them) so he figured that the *best* way to sort things was to **kill off** *all* the **new-born baby boys**. *That* should do it.

One mum decided *not* to play ball and kept her baby boy hidden (and quiet!). But when she could hide him no longer she manufactured a **basket-boat** made out of reeds and put her son (Moses as he was *later* called) into it ...

A RUBBER DINGHY WOULD HAVE BEEN EASIER, BUT THEY'VE NOT BEEN INVENTED YET!

Moses' mum placed the basket-boat into the River Nile and ... Well, I'm not going to tell you how the story ends but Bible book **Exodus chapter 2** from **verses 4** to **10** *will*.

CHRISTMAS

The *good* thing about the Bible is that it's packed with loads of info and *sometimes* you can read the same story in *more* than one Bible book. *That's* what you get with the **Christmas story**. You get *one* lot of info from a guy called **Matthew** and a whole heap of *other* stuff from a writer called **Luke**. Put them both together and you've got the familiar Christmas story. But for now, let's head off to Bible book **Matthew chapter 1** and **verse 18** onward to check out *his* version of the events.

Jesus's mum (**Mary**) was getting ready to marry a guy called **Joseph** when an **angel from God** informed her that God was going to make her pregnant with a very *special* child who was going to sort out the world's sin problem. Mary said she'd agree to this and Joseph agreed he'd still marry Mary and so, in due course, Jesus was born in **Bethlehem**.

Matthew tells us that some important men from the **east** came to visit God's special Son but this was quite a while *after* the birth. To discover who came visiting on the very *night* of Jesus's birth you'll need to skip to Luke's account in **Luke chapter 2**. See if you can find *who* dropped in to worship Jesus. Here's a clue ...

OI! YOU'RE NOT MEANT TO BE HERE UNTIL LATER IN THE STORY!

EASTER

A lot of people seem to have the idea that **Jesus's death** was a bit of an unfortunate mistake. That's complete *nonsense*, in fact it couldn't be *further* from the truth. Jesus was *forever* telling his disciples that he was making tracks for Jerusalem where he was gonna be **executed**. It was all part of **God's plan**. We haven't got much space to pack in all you need to know about the Easter story but basically, Jesus gets arrested in **Jerusalem** by the jealous religious leaders (and the Romans) and **stitched up** then he's sent for trial.

Result:**The death sentence.**

After being flogged, beaten, mocked and spat upon Jesus is hung up to die on a **wooden cross** with nails in his hands and feet.

While Jesus's life ebbed away, the Roman guards gambled for his clothes. And then, just before he breathed his last, the sky went **black** (and stayed that way for three hours!).

Then Jesus died.

Immediately, some awesome things happened.

There was an **earthquake**, the **huge curtain** in the Temple was torn in two and **dead people** came back to life from their graves.

Something out of this world was going on before everyone's eyes. But that was *just* the **beginning**. Have a read of **Matthew chapter 27** starting at **verse 57** and finishing at **chapter 28 verse 10** and you'll find out whether that really *was* the end of Jesus.

HARD LUCK STORIES

Nowadays there's nothing *worse* than for a **celebrity** to have the nasty bits of their lives splashed across the newspapers and magazines. Well *that's* rather like what **Job** (usually pronounced '*Jobe*') had to put up with. He's got **42 chapters** of the Bible dedicated to his **misery** and **woe**.

To be fair, the Bible tells us that Job was a man who **worshipped God** and was **faithful** to him.

He was *also* **stinking rich** ...

WITH THE EMPHASIS ON STINKING!

But the **Devil** (God's enemy) had his sights well and truly trained on this good man. *He* wanted to find out if Job would think *quite* so highly of God if things weren't going *quite* so well. One by one, the Devil brought a whole *bunch* of **calamities** on Job's family and possessions until (bit by bit) they were all **wiped out**.

With nothing left but his health, the Devil inflicted Job with the **world's horriblest skin disease** (weeping sores etc). It was *so* bad that even his *friends* didn't recognise him.

The three of them did their *best* to persuade Job that he *must* have done something **bad** but Job was having *none* of it.

He stuck up for God and in the end God stuck up for *him* by healing him, making him stinking rich again and giving him a new family. The Devil was **outsmarted by Job** because Job *never* gave up on God. Have a look what Job has to say at the end of his terrible ordeal in **Job chapter 42 verse 5**.

WEDDINGS

This must be just about the most **unusual wedding** you've *ever* read about and let me tell you *why*. For starters, the location *isn't* a **pretty church** for the service and then a **nice hotel** for the reception. Nope! This one's definitely *not* a chauffeur-driven car ride away. To be blunt, unless you make it to heaven then you're **not invited**. So, what's it all about? Well, *this* Bible bit occurs right near the very *end* of the Bible and it's all about a **wedding** between **Jesus** and the **church**. That's because the Bible calls the church (that's everyone who's a Christian) the **bride of Christ**. There's going to come a time when Jesus's people get together with Jesus so that they can be with him forever. Just like a marriage is meant to be. In the Bible book of **Revelation** (where *this* bit comes from) it says that Jesus's bride has got to get **ready** for this wedding just like a *real* bride would. You'd hardly expect a bride to be off doing her week's shopping or having a girls' night out on her wedding day, would you? (Well hopefully not!).

I'M SURE I'M MEANT TO BE DOING SOMETHING SPECIAL BUT I CAN'T REMEMBER WHAT IT IS!

So that means *always* living your life as if you're about to meet up with Jesus (your bridegroom). You've gotta be **ready**! What will Jesus's bride be given if she is ready and waiting? Have a peek in **Revelation chapter 19** and **verse 8**.

VICTORIES

As **Winnie the Pooh** knew full well, putting your paw inside a **beehive** is *guaranteed* to set those bees a-buzzing. **Gideon**, the star of *this* Bible story, had just stirred up the **Midianites** and they were now out to get him and his people (the Israelites).

Gideon had *only* been doing what **God** had *told* him to do which was to destroy an altar to the Midianite god **Baal**. And *now* he had a war on his hands. Not only *that* but Gideon couldn't see why on *earth* God had chosen *him* to **lead the Israelites**. As far as *he* was concerned he was just a *nothing*. Don't worry Gideon, that's all part of God's plan!

When Gideon had assembled his army God said a surprising thing. He didn't say that it was too small ... he said it was **too big**! (**Thirty-two thousand men**, for those of you interested in *statistics*). God instructed Gideon to send home anyone who was **afraid** ... which left him with **10,000** men.

God set *this* lot a special test (read the *full* story to find out *what* it was) which whittled Gideon's army down to ... **300**!

The Bible tells us that Gideon's enemies were spread out like a **swarm of locusts** and that they had as many **camels** as there were **grains on the seashore**.

How on *earth* could Gideon and just 300 men defeat *this* lot? **Judges chapter 7** from **verse 19** to **25** has your answer.

VICTORIES

We've featured good old **Elijah** elsewhere in this Boring Bible book, but *this* story about his head to head with the **prophets of Baal** is simply *too* good to miss.

After a two to three year **drought** (Elijah had commanded the rain to stop) Israel was about to get rain again. Wicked king **Ahab** and his *equally* wicked wife, **Jezebel**, were part of the *reason* for God's punishment on the land. They, along with *most* of the people, worshipped the god Baal (and any *other* gods that they took a shine to – but *not* the **Lord God**).

Elijah was going to show this stubborn nation who really *was* **boss**. He got everyone up on to **Mount Carmel** for a **showdown**. *Everyone* included **450** prophets of Baal and **400** prophets of the goddess Asherah.

Elijah had **two bulls** cut to pieces and laid on some **wood** for the prophets to sacrifice to their gods. All good sacrifices need to be burned so Elijah challenged the prophets of Baal to call upon their god to **set it alight**. The prophets duly obliged and started dancing around the altar and shouted out to their god to send fire. Their ranting and raving continued all through the day while Elijah stood by, taunting them ...

You're gonna need to read the big ending to this awesome story yourself in **1 Kings chapter 18** from **verse 30** to **46**. It's a *brilliant* story so make *sure* you head there **right now**!

DEFEATS

Things had gone from *bad* to *worse* with God's people (the Israelites) and they'd *even* ended up fighting against themselves so that there was a **big split**. The city of **Jerusalem** was ruled by the **kings of Judah**, but one king after another, they sinned against God. Enough was enough and God called time on their **wicked ways** by sending the **Babylonian army** to attack them – in two stages.

Stage *one* was where eighteen-year-old **King Jehoiachin** (and 7,000 others) were deported to Babylon.

King Nebuchadnezzar then made Jehoiachin's uncle king (Mattaniah, who *then* changed his name to **Zedekiah**) but he was as *bad* as the *rest* of them and simply made things worse by rebelling against Nebuchadnezzar. *Not* a wise thing to do. Back came the Babylonian army but *this* time they besieged the city of Jerusalem for so long that all the food ran out ...

WE COULD ALWAYS SEND OUT FOR A PIZZA I SUPPOSE!

Jerusalem was virtually **destroyed** and *this* time just about everyone was carted off to captivity in Babylon.

Not only *that* but Zedekiah had his **eyes gouged out** (ouch!!!). As for King Jehoiachin, well there was a *bit* of a happy ending for him but he had to wait **37** years for it, as you'll see in **2 Kings chapter 25 verses 27** through to **30**.

WIVES

King Solomon had *everything* going for him. He had **wisdom**, and **wealth** in abundance but he also had something *else* in abundance beginning with 'w' and that was **wives**. I'll tell you how *many* wives he had in a moment but *one* thing's for sure – having as many wives as Solomon had was **not good** ...

ALL THESE WEDDING ANNIVERSARIES TO REMEMBER!

Er, that's not *quite* what I was thinking of.

What I was *meaning* was that **God** had warned **Solomon** that on **no account** was he to marry women from the nations surrounding Israel. *They* worshipped *other* gods and if *they* were allowed into the royal palace they'd bring with them all their **detestable idols**. Did Solomon heed God's warning? Well, amazingly *not*. Which is quite astounding because the Bible tells us that Solomon had actually *met* God **twice**.

So, how many wives did king Solomom have? A cool **700**! But that wasn't the end of it, **no way**! He also had **300** concubines (which are sort of live-in lovers). *That* makes a whopping **one thousand** wives in total.

How did God respond to Solomon's disobedience?

Read **1 Kings chapter 11** from **verse 9** through to **verse 11**.

DESTRUCTION

One thing's for sure, it's that everyone reading this book lives in *one* country or *another*. If you live in somewhere like England then you're part of the **United Kingdom**. Jesus made a *big thing* about **kingdoms** and he said that there were really only actually **two kingdoms** that you needed to know about. *One* was the **kingdom of God** which is *everything* to do with Jesus being king of your life and the *other* is the **kingdom of this world**. *That* one is ruled by God's enemy, the **Devil** and is opposed to *everything* that God stands for.

This kingdom also sometimes goes by the name of **Babylon** and represents *all* the **wicked things** people do when they turn their backs on God. But in the Bible book **Revelation** there's a big bit about how one day God is going to **punish** this evil kingdom by **destroying it completely**.

Why does God want to destroy it? Because he knows that when people turn their backs on him they only live to please themselves, which means they hurt *other* people. *That* was never, *ever* God's plan for human beings. God wants the *best* for us but if you search through Bible book **Revelation chapter 18** and look at **verses 9** to **17** you'll soon see that *some* people will actually be *sad* when God destroys the Devil's wicked kingdom.

INSTRUCTION

Most people (if they're honest,) don't *really* like being told what to do. That's usually 'cos we think that *we* know best. We think that rules and instructions are just made up to give us a hard time and to **spoil our fun** ...

This Bible bit checks out some rules that **God** gave **people** to make their lives *better* but (a lot like us) the people God *gave* them to thought that he was be just being a bit of a **spoilsport**.

What sort of instructions were they? Well, pretty *obvious* things like **don't kill other human beings** or **steal from them**.

You've probably heard of them, they're called the **Ten Commandments** ('cos there's ten of them – surprise, surprise!). How did God let on what they were? Easy! A guy called Moses collected them from God (up a mountain) and they were written down on **stone slabs**.

All ten are listed down in **Exodus chapter 20 verse 1** through to **17**. You'll soon see that they all make good sense and stop us human beings from getting hurt (and hurting each other).

But there's *one* intruction that's got a bit of a **promise** added on to it. Go and find out what you get for keeping commandment **number 5 – verse 12** will tell all.

(Then how about trying to obey it!!!)

QUICK EXITS

There are **two** guys in the Bible who have the *same* claim to fame and *one* of them is our good friend **Elijah**. Elijah was what you'd call a **top prophet of God** and wherever he went miraculous things seemed to happen. His last day on earth was *extraordinary* to say the least. He'd been told by God to head for a place called Bethel and **Elisha** (his second-in-command) was *determined* to go with him.

On the way they met a whole bunch of *other* prophets of God (**fifty** in all) in the various towns that they passed through. *Each* time they kept telling Elisha that today was the day that Elijah was **leaving earth**. And *each* time Elisha came back with the same reply ...

Just before Elijah went to be with God he asked Elisha if he had any last requests.

Elisha asked for **Elijah's power** so he could carry on where Elijah left off. Elijah agreed on the condition that Elisha *saw* him being taken away. *Did* Elisha get what he asked for and how *exactly* did Elijah go? Answers in **2 Kings chapter 2 verse 11** and **12**. You'll discover that Elijah's claim to fame was that he never *actually* **died** before he went to be with God, but to find out with who *else* he shared this claim to fame, turn to **Genesis chapter 5 verses 22** to **24**.

SUPERMEN

As you've probably picked up by now (*if* you've being paying attention) the Israelites were more often than not at war with somebody or other. Right now, in *this* Bible bit, their enemies are the **Philistines** (boo! hiss!) who are making life perfectly **horrid** for them. **Samson** (their leader) had the job of getting the Philistines off Israel's back and giving them a break. Before he was born, an angel from God had turned up to tell Samson's mum that he must never, *ever* have his **hair cut**, as a sign that his life was **dedicated to God**. Samson grew up to be a strapping chap with **super-human strength**. He thought *nothing* of tearing a **lion** apart with his bare hands or killing **thirty young men** single-handed. But should his hair *ever* get cut then he could **wave goodbye** to his **super powers**. It's a pity he didn't save *some* of his power for making wise decisions, because one day he let slip to his Philistine wife (**Delilah**) about the secret of his strength. The long and the short of it was that some Philistines cut his **long** hair **short** – and with it went Samson's super powers ...

ANY CHANCE OF A SPOT OF HAIR GEL?

The Philistines thought they'd had the **last laugh** but they should have known *better*. While Samson was banged up in prison his hair began to *grow* again – and with it his **strength**. Go to **Judges chapter 16** and read from **verse 23** to **verse 31** to find out how Samson used his new-found strength.

WRESTLING

"**Pick on someone your own size!**" That's what you say to someone bigger than you when they're trying to annoy you. But **Jacob** (the main man in *this* Bible bit) did the complete *opposite*. *He* picked on someone **bigger** than *himself* and *that* person was **God**. When I say *bigger*, I don't particularly mean how *tall* they were. It's just that God is, well, *God* and *that* means he's got all the power of heaven at his fingertips. How did this tussle with God come about? Well it's a long story but, in short, Jacob was going home after years of being on the run. God had given him the job of taking over from his dad (**Isaac**) and heading up the **Israelite nation**. Up 'till now, Jacob had *struggled* to live a life that pleased God – let's be honest, he'd been **downright devious**! Nevertheless, Jacob was God's **chosen man**, but *first* he needed to come into line with God. One night, Jacob just *couldn't* sleep (probably worried about being Israel's leader). While he was tossing and turning, a **man** showed up and started a **wresting match** with Jacob. Jacob gave as good as he got and

I WON'T LET GO UNTIL YOU BLESS ME!

held on to his opponent with all his strength. The man, so it turned out, was **God** (or perhaps an angel from God). It was as if Jacob had *finally* twigged that rather than keep *running* from God he needed to hold on *tight* to him. In the thick of the fight Jacob's **hip** was thrown out of joint and he was left with a **limp** that would be a permanent reminder of his wrestling match with God. Something a bit *less* painful *also* happened to Jacob which can be looked up in **Genesis chapter 32 verse 28**.

WITCHES

This very *last* Bible bit is a stark warning that **disobeying God** is *not* a good move. **King Saul of Israel** had made a complete *mess* of things and the prophet **Samuel** had told Saul that God was no longer going to be with him. He was **on his own**. *That* meant that when he went into battle he could only expect **terrible defeats**. To make matters *worse*, the **Philistine army** were preparing to *attack* Israel. Things were looking very bleak for Saul and he made one last ditch effort to find out from God what he should do. But the line was dead. God said nothing. So Saul did a stupid thing. He went to see a **witch** in a place called **Endor**. Why was that stupid? Easy. Witches got their powers from none other than God's enemy, the Devil. God had **forbidden** the Israelites from having *anything* to do with the likes of witches ... **or they would face the consequences.** Saul thought he could outsmart God by disguising himself as a woman so he wouldn't be recognised But the witch saw through Saul's charade ...

I KNEW I SHOULD HAVE SHAVED!

... and *so* did God. He sent a **vision** of the **prophet Samuel** to tell Saul that his time was up and that the very next day he would be **dead**. End of story.

This *whole* story can be found in Bible book **1 Samuel chapter 28** but to find out *how* king Saul met his end you'll need to skip forward a page or two to **1 Samuel chapter 31** (all of it!).

Well, that just about wraps it up for *this* Boring Bible book.
I hope you enjoyed it and found it helpful.

To be honest, it's been really hard trying to decide *what* to put in *Bible Buster* 'cos it's meant we've had to leave out loads and loads of *other* brilliant Bible bits that we'd have loved to have introduced you to.

But now you've got the hang of getting stuck into the Bible why not do a bit of exploring on your own?

Something like Bible book **Mark** would be a good place to start 'cos it'll give you a **whirlwind tour of Jesus's life**.

Or maybe you could whiz to **Exodus** and read up the whole story of **Moses** and all the **amazing miracles** that seemed to follow him round.

And if you've got a birthday coming up, why not ask for something like a **Bible handbook** which is a book that will tell you loads and loads of fascinating info about the Bible that we've not had space for.

Either way, *whatever* you do, don't *stop* reading the Bible now that you've *started*.

Bit by bit you'll start to see what a **brilliant God**, God is.

Happy reading!

See ya!